ROCKSTAR SUCCESS STORIES

ROCKSTAR SUCCESS STORIES

INSPIRATIONAL STORIES OF SUCCESS BY
EXTRAORDINARY "ROCKSTARS"

CRAIG DUSWALT

New York

Publishing Professional Books and Products for *RockStar Entrepreneurs*

ROCKSTAR SUCCESS STORIES

Inspirational Stories Of Success By Extraordinary "Rockstars"

© 2016 CRAIG DUSWALT.

Published in New York, New York, by Morgan James Publishing. Morgan James and The Entrepreneurial Publisher are trademarks of Morgan James, LLC. www.MorganJamesPublishing.com

The Morgan James Speakers Group can bring authors to your live event. For more information or to book an event visit The Morgan James Speakers Group at www.TheMorganJamesSpeakersGroup.com.

Co-Publisher Duswalt Press

Shelfie

A free eBook edition is available with the purchase of this print book.

CLEARLY PRINT YOUR NAME ABOVE IN UPPER CASE

Instructions to claim your free eBook edition:
1. Download the Shelfie app for Android or iOS
2. Write your name in UPPER CASE above
3. Use the Shelfie app to submit a photo
4. Download your eBook to any device

ISBN 978-1-63047-921-3 paperback
ISBN 978-1-63047-922-0 eBook
Library of Congress Control Number:
2016900189

Photo of Craig Duswalt by:
Robert John Craig

Cover Design by:
Chris Treccani
www.3dogdesign.net

Interior Design by:
Bonnie Bushman
The Whole Caboodle Graphic Design

In an effort to support local communities and raise awareness and funds, Morgan James Publishing donates a percentage of all book sales for the life of each book to Habitat for Humanity Peninsula and Greater Williamsburg.

Get involved today, visit
www.MorganJamesBuilds.com

Habitat for Humanity®
Peninsula and
Greater Williamsburg
Building Partner

DEDICATION

This book is dedicated to all the dreamers out there who never give up and continue to strive for success. Embrace your "RockStar" life.

TABLE OF CONTENTS

INTRODUCTION

In my opinion, there are many different types of RockStars in the world. Of course, there's the RockStar that we all recognize as RockStars in the music industry. But there are also many people who are very successful in their specific industry, and in my opinion, they are RockStars as well.

RockStar Success Stories is filled with these people. A couple of them happen to be household names. Most of them are not. But they all had some form of success in their lives, and I am honored to share their stories with you.

Success does not necessarily mean more money, or a high-profile job, or a big house, or an expensive car. As you will see when you read these stories, success can be a simple change of mindset, a realization, a cure of a disease, more freedom, following a passion, a lucky break because you worked hard, triumph of the human spirit, and yes, sometimes it can mean more money.

I personally speak to corporations, entrepreneur conferences, author conferences, social media conferences, personal development conferences, associations, networking groups, colleges, and even youth groups, and I meet tons of amazing people, and I hear the most incredible stories of success. Their stories inspire me to become a better person, a better husband, and a better father. They also inspire me to want to become more successful in my business, and so I felt these stories were important to share.

This is the first book in the *RockStar Success Stories* series. But there are still so many more wonderful "RockStar" stories to fill hundreds of books, and we plan to do exactly that so we can get as many powerful messages out to the world as possible.

Read one story a day, or read the entire book over a few days. You will begin to believe that anything is possible, and that you can be a "RockStar" as well.

Thank you to all the wonderful authors of this book. Thank you for your time, your energy, and for sharing your story of success.

Craig Duswalt

THE NIGHT THAT CHANGED MY LIFE

by Craig Duswalt

I t was July 1983. I had just graduated college—State University of New York at Oswego. I was a business major with a theatre minor, but I was very involved in theatre. I had starred in numerous college productions in my junior and senior years. Acting was in my blood forever.

My first job out of college was at the Westbury Music Fair in Long Island, New York. Westbury Music Fair was a 3,000-seat, in-the-round venue that housed plays and intimate concerts. I was a backstage runner, a gopher, the bottom man on the totem pole. When acts came into town, I would pick them up at the airport. Or, I would pick them up at their hotel, and bring them to the gig for sound check. And I always had to make sure they had what they needed backstage.

I only held this job for about a month, because I was about to meet someone who would change my life.

The Australian pop band, Air Supply, came to Westbury Music Fair to do two shows—one on Friday night and one on Saturday night.

What I did not know at the time was that Air Supply had just fired their band assistant because of excessive drug use.

I worked the show on Friday night, getting drinks, supplying towels, etc. I met the two lead members of the band, Russell Hitchcock and Graham Russell, as well as their security guard, Bob Street. Nothing special, just "Hi!" and some small talk. But I was working my butt off

1

that night, running around for everyone—but always with a smile and a positive attitude.

The next day I found out my mom and her friend had tickets to see Air Supply that night. I wasn't supposed to work that night but because my mom was going I asked my boss if I could come in again to work the second show.

Two weeks earlier, out of nowhere, knowing that Air Supply was coming to town, my mom said to me, "What if they ask you to go on tour with them, would you go?"

I said, "Who?"

"Air Supply, what if they ask you to tour with them?"

I said to my Mom, "And why would they do that? You're crazy! Where do you come up with this stuff?"

I never gave it another thought.

I arrived at work about 2:00 p.m. to help get things ready for the Saturday night show. At about 5:00 p.m., Air Supply arrived to do a sound check. Once again, there were casual hellos from the band members. But Bob Street talked to me a little about my interests, and how I liked working at Westbury. About a half hour later Bob and the band went back to the hotel to rest before the show.

The concert was sold out.

As I got the backstage area ready, the excited crowd took their seats. About an hour later the warm-up band took the stage. I peeked out from behind the backstage curtain, and saw my mom and her friend in the audience.

Air Supply arrived through the Stage Door entrance. As the band members went to their dressing rooms, Bob Street pulled me aside and asked me how much I made working at Westbury. I told him about $150 a week. (Don't laugh. Back in 1983, $150 a week wasn't bad).

Bob said, "Do you want to quadruple that?"

So many things went through my mind at that moment, one of them being, "What the hell does he want me to do to make $600 a week?"

My mind went to some very dark places. But I was 21 years old—and I was thinking to myself, "Hell, whatever he says, I'll do it." I wouldn't really, but that's what I was thinking.

So I said, "Hell yeah... doing what?"

I was told that they needed a person to take care of the band and their backstage area while they were on the road. They liked the way I worked, they liked my positive attitude and they loved my energy, so they wanted to offer me a job to join them on their world tour.

I was in shock. I think I said, "When do I leave?"

Bob said, "Come to our hotel tomorrow to iron out the details with our tour manager, John Slattery."

We shook hands and he went into a dressing room. I stood there dumbfounded, wondering what the hell just happened. Did I just get a job touring with one of the biggest pop bands in the world?

You bet I did. I would be leaving on Monday for a world tour with Air Supply, one of the most successful bands of the 1980's. And then I realized what my mom had said to me two weeks ago.

Holy crap—my mom's a psychic!

I was busting to tell the world what just happened. When the warm-up band finished I very coolly walk over to where my mom and her friend were sitting in the audience.

I casually said to my mom, "Do you remember what you asked me two weeks ago?"

She did not recall. (There goes the "my mom's a psychic" theory.)

"About touring with Air Supply," I reminded her.

"Oh yeah."

"Well, as crazy as this sounds, you were right."

"What are you talking about?"

"They asked me to tour with them. I leave on Monday."

At first my mom let out a small squeal, so as to not freak out or scare the other 3,000 people in the theatre. But then she realized what was happening and got really excited.

As I left her to return backstage I heard another squeal.

Again, it was her.

I just lowered my head and rushed behind the backstage curtain.

The next day I came back to the band's hotel and met with John Slattery, and I was "officially" hired on the spot. That night I called all my friends from Deer Park, NY and I threw my own last-minute going away party.

The band sent a limo to my house the next morning, and it took me to JFK Airport. I hopped on a flight to Wallingford, CT, checked into the hotel, rode with the band to the venue and watched them take the stage. As I watched the concert from the side of the stage I just remember thinking to myself, WOW! This is going to be very, very cool. And it was.

I toured with Air Supply for six amazing years. They all remain great friends of mine to this day.

In all my seminars, I talk about always doing your best, just in case someone's watching. That's what I did that night, and that's what I do every day. A positive attitude, great energy and always smiling—that is the key to success.

―――――――

Craig Duswalt is a professional speaker, author, radio host and creator of Craig Duswalt Marketing—How to Achieve RockStar Status in Your Industry. His background includes touring with Guns N' Roses, as Axl Rose's personal assistant, and Air Supply, as the band's personal assistant.

Craig was also an award-winning copywriter, working as a Senior Copywriter for a Los Angeles-based ad agency until opening up his own ad agency, Green Room Design and Advertising, which was named the 2002 Santa Clarita Valley Chamber of Commerce Small Business of the Year.

Craig combined his backgrounds in both music and marketing and is known in the industry for putting on amazing 3-Day Marketing BootCamps every March and September in Los Angeles, and 3-Day Personal Growth Weekends every January, also in Los Angeles.

Craig speaks to entrepreneurs, small business owners, corporations and colleges on how to stand out from the competition by thinking like a RockStar.

www.CraigDuswaltMarketing.com

ENJOY SUCCESS BUT ALWAYS KEEP YOUR FAMILY A TOP PRIORITY!

by James Malinchak

M ost people have an inspiration in their life. Maybe it's a talk with someone you respect or an experience. Whatever the inspiration, it tends to make you look at life from a different perspective.

My inspiration came from my sister Vicki, a kind and caring person. She didn't care about accolades or being written about in newspapers. All she wanted was to share her love with the people she cared about, her family and friends.

The summer before my junior year of college, I received a phone call from my father saying that Vicki had been rushed to the hospital. She had collapsed, and the right side of her body was paralyzed. The preliminary indications were that she had suffered a stroke. However, test results confirmed it was much more serious.

There was a malignant brain tumor causing her paralysis. Doctors didn't give her more than three months to live. I remember wondering how this could happen. The day before, Vicki was perfectly fine. Now, her life was coming to an end at such a young age.

After overcoming the initial shock and feeling of emptiness, I decided that Vicki needed hope and encouragement. She needed someone to make her believe that she could overcome this obstacle. I became Vicki's coach.

Every day we would visualize the tumor shrinking, and everything that we talked about was positive. I even posted a sign on her hospital room door that read, "If you have any negative thoughts, leave them at the door." I was determined to help Vicki beat the tumor. She and I made a deal that we called 50-50. I would do 50% of the fighting, and Vicki would do the other 50%.

The month of August arrived, and it was time to begin my junior year of college 3,000 miles away. I was unsure whether I should leave or stay with Vicki. I made the mistake of telling her that I might not leave for school. She became angry and said not to worry because she would be fine.

There was Vicki lying ill in a hospital bed telling me not to worry. I realized that if I stayed it might send a message that she was dying, and I didn't want her believing that. Vicki needed to believe that she could win against the tumor.

Leaving that night feeling it might be the last time I would ever see Vicki alive was the most difficult thing I have ever done in my entire life. While at school, I never stopped fighting my 50% for her. Every night before falling asleep, I would look through my bedroom window, up into the dark sky, and I would talk to Vicki, hoping that there was some way she could hear me. I would say, "Vicki, I'm fighting for you, and I will never quit. As long as you never quit fighting, we will beat this."

A few months passed, and she was still holding on. I was talking with an elderly friend, and she asked about Vicki's situation. I told her that she was getting worse but that she wasn't quitting. My friend asked a question that really made me think. She said, "Do you think the reason she hasn't let go is because she doesn't want to let you down?"

Maybe she was right? Maybe I was selfish for encouraging Vicki to keep fighting? That night before falling asleep, I once again did what I had done every night for a few months. I looked through my bedroom window, up into the dark sky, and talked to Vicki. I said to her, "Vicki, I understand that you're in a lot of pain and that you may like to let go. If you do, then I want you to. We didn't lose because you never quit fighting. If you want to go on to a better place, then I understand. We will be together again. I love you, and I'll always be with you wherever you are."

Early the next morning, my mother called to tell me that Vicki had passed away.

WOW!

I've often thought a lot about that experience with Vicki, and while it was an extremely sad time for my family, Vicki's passing away changed my life! She is one of the main reasons I started speaking for corporations, associations, business groups, colleges, and universities in America and internationally, sharing a message of hope, inspiration, and encouragement.

Vicki serves as my inspiration as a professional speaker. It's amazing! Out of all the stories I share from the stage in my presentations, more people approach me after, thanking me for sharing "Vicki's story" than any other story, success strategy, or humorous joke.

That's why I love sharing her story. Not only does it inspire people to live a more thankful, grateful, and abundant life, but it also allows me to turn that sad moment into a voice that uplifts and inspires, not only myself, but others.

I hope sharing Vicki's story helps you to think about how blessed you are to have good health, safety, and peace in life for yourself and your family! I also hope that it will serve as an inspiration for you that if ever a challenging time arises in your life, you CAN get through it and can allow that moment to serve as a message of hope, inspiration, and encouragement for others.

Go out and be a voice that uplifts and inspires someone's life today!

One thing we should always be thankful for is our families. Printed below is a poem that I wrote. I hope you enjoy it and will share it with your family.

Thank You Family

For teaching me wrong from right
And for encouraging me to keep my dreams in sight
For showing me not to let obstacles keep me down
And for creating a smile from my frown
For saying that you care about me
And for showing just how special love should be
For wiping my tears away when I'm feeling sad
And for calming me down when I tend to get mad
For helping others with the good that you do
And for teaching me that I should help others, too
For hugging me when I'm feeling blue
And whispering into my ear "I love you"
Thank you, family, for all that you do
I don't know where I would be if it weren't for you

James Malinchak is recognized as one of the most requested, in-demand business and motivational keynote speakers and marketing consultants in the world. He was featured on the Hit ABC TV Show, Secret Millionaire and was twice named College Speaker of the Year. James has delivered over 2,000+ presentations for corporations, associations, business groups, colleges, universities and youth organizations worldwide. James can speak for groups ranging from 20 - 20,000.

www.Malinchak.com

WORKFORCE REDUCTION INTO LEMONADE

by Derrick Hall

I t can be an absolute challenge to feel like a RockStar with your employees when they know economic conditions have forced the organization to analyze the necessity of all full-time positions. This was the setting in 2008, when Arizona was experiencing one of its worst economic downturns in decades. With over 350 full-time staff members at the time, I realized the fiscally responsible action was to assess all levels and determine which jobs could be combined and which could ultimately be eliminated.

This was a daunting task for a Team President who had prided himself on the award-winning culture that had been created. Each and every one of my employees was like a member of my own family to me, as well as to my wife, Amy. After weeks of consultant engagement and internal interviews, it had been decided that 40 positions could be abolished, the largest workplace reduction in the history of our organization.

With such a sensitive topic and people's livelihoods at stake, this information was kept confidential and between just a few of my key executives. This made it perhaps even worse. There were few I could talk to in order to fully process the accuracy of our findings. The non-stop questions kept ringing in my head—"Was this totally necessary?" "What if the economy recovers tomorrow?" "Should we enforce furloughs instead?" "Am I identifying the proper individuals?" There were sleepless nights and hour-long tearful conversations each night at home with my better half. I could not look close friends in the eyes leading up to the reduction, knowing that I was sending them out the door in need of new jobs.

The Friday came when it was time to take action, and we did so in a very respectful and dignified fashion, giving these innocent and hardworking loyalists a way to exit with their heads held high and enough to make ends meet while they search for their next career moves. And we eliminated jobs across the board, not just at the lower or entry levels. There were managers, directors, senior directors, and even vice presidents from my leadership team who all fell victim to this swift and appropriate plan. It was the most difficult day in my professional career.

When the dust settled days later, and those who survived realized and trusted there would be no further cuts or waves, what could have been an extremely negative time for this franchise became one of hope and belief in its leaders. The feedback was in direct contrast to how I had envisioned the outcome. Our staff actually respected the decisions that we had made and were confident that they were made objectively and without favoritism. I was also told on several occasions that the employees could tell how deeply moved and saddened I was by the process.

The Arizona Diamondbacks culture was actually strengthened during these days that I had deemed so dark. Remaining employees thanked me for having faith in their abilities and made promises to make us proud. A tight-knit group got even closer, and the overall mission was in focus sharper than ever before.

Those few who joined me in the miserable task of eliminating positions and negatively impacting some lives were now considered Rock Stars by the staff—for analyzing the entire organization thoroughly enough and without bias and making decisions that all could universally get behind and never question.

In our positions, we will be forced to make choices that will not always be favorable or popular. But if we remain fair, consistent, and honest, our integrity will always stay intact, and our fiduciary responsibilities will forever be fulfilled.

Considered by many to be among the leaders of the game, Arizona Diamondbacks President & CEO Derrick Hall has turned the D-backs into a model franchise within the sports industry and throughout the business world during his ten years at the helm of the club. Hall focuses the organization's efforts in five areas he has called the "Circle of Success"—fan experience, performance, community, culture, and financial efficiency—each of which has seen tremendous success during his tenure.

The D-backs were recently named the No. 1 franchise in baseball and No. 6 in all of sports by *ESPN the Magazine* based on eight categories on and off the field. Among his most significant accomplishments during his tenure as President & CEO has been the opening of Salt River Fields at Talking Stick, the D-backs' Spring Training home in Scottsdale; hosting the 2011 Major League All-Star Game at Chase Field for the first time ever; two division titles, one in 2007 and another in 2011, an NLCS appearance and the hiring of Hall of Fame manager Tony La Russa as Chief Baseball Officer to oversee the team's baseball operations; the positioning of the D-backs as one of the largest philanthropic entities in the Valley, having recently surpassed $45 million in charitable giving since the team's inception in 1998, including more than $5.5 million last season; and the creation of a corporate culture that led Yahoo! to deem the club as "the best workplace in sports."

www.dbacks.com

THOUGHTS AND WORDS

by Natasha Duswalt

Our thoughts and words are infinite in what they create and produce. I started modeling at the age of seventeen, and traveled around the world and realized that I wanted something else, but the beliefs I had formed around my career were limiting my growth. Somewhere the lines were blurred and my personal value was based on how I looked, how my photos turned out, what size I was wearing and what clients I was booking. Don't get me wrong I had a great ride and I would not change it for the world. I loved the industry but wanted to have longevity. The trick was, what's the next step?

That question brought me to start my own modeling agency, Peak Models & Talent in Los Angeles. I had recently attended a Tony Robbins seminar and I made a decision, formed out of a thought, backed with passion and directed by a vision, to own my own business.

Even though my mind was riddled with doubt, I was able to apply all of the skills that I had picked up while modeling and parlayed that into a company where I am able to help others on a daily basis.

The thoughts and words we have behind the scenes of our lives need to be monitored in order to succeed.

To overcome fear and doubt my background mantra was to always be of service to anyone that I encountered. However, after many years I found that the responsibility of the agency was wearing me down, and I was about to face a new challenge that I certainly was not expecting…ever.

In October 2006 I was told by a doctor that I had Hodgkin's Lymphoma, a blood cancer. At that moment all I could think was, "What does this mean? Am I going to die? What will my children and husband do without me?" All of the thoughts came racing at me like a train through my head—unstoppable, fearful, terrifying, and completely unhappy thoughts. My reaction was tears. Tears for the kids that I brought into this world to take care of; tears for a husband that married me to have a family with; tears for me that I might have to knowingly go down a path that could possibly result in my mortal end. All of this was overwhelming and painful.

My thoughts were taking control of my existence. This is what happens when we face life on life's terms. After battling the thoughts of despair, I finally took control of my thoughts and words. Cancer might have sucker-punched me at first, but I needed to gain control of my life again.

Every day I started to focus on living. Living meant doing the things I wanted to do in–between doctor visits and treatments. Living meant envisioning myself with my kids and husband well after this part of my life was over. My choice was to see my life after cancer, not to stay in the fear. My life needed to be focused on faith. The faith that I could do this, and the faith that God was with me and wanted me to continue living.

Contrary to popular belief, I was not "fighting" cancer, I was surrendering control over to God because the idea of "fighting" cancer was too big of a battle to do alone. The point is—that no matter what happens we get to take control of our thoughts and words. My diagnosis was just that—a diagnosis that just happened to require medical care.

I decided, after surrendering, that this was nothing more than a small problem that would pass through my life, and that was it. I stopped focusing on the negative and instead focused on the fact that this would soon be over. When people asked about my illness I simply told them that I was "diagnosed," meaning that it was someone else's opinion that I was being treated for cancer—not mine.

Do you see how different that is?

Most people say they have cancer. I personally believe that this is not helpful. I never owned the "C" word.

After 12 rounds of chemo I was finished with the process, and I was ready to move on.

I have been called a survivor. That is one label for it. People also ask me if I'm in remission, but I believe remission implies that it is still possibly there. I prefer to say I was cured of a diagnosis back in 2006.

The rest is history. Life wanted me back in full force, living a life of purpose…on purpose.

The thoughts and words you choose to use in your daily life are very powerful and with a few changes in your daily dialogue you will notice that you feel better every day. We all have those moments where we question everything.

When someone asks you how your day is going, think positive! If you are not in the hospital you are GREAT! The bottom line is that you get to choose the thoughts you think and the words you use, and it feels much better to choose empowering words everywhere you go with every person you encounter.

Remember that everyone you meet is probably struggling with thoughts and feelings just as you are. Giving them something positive to think about or a kind word can really lift their spirits.

One of my favorite things to do is to ask them a question that might get them thinking of something wonderful they could be doing.

The power of thought is immeasurable. The power of our words and language shapes our feelings and outcomes as a person.

Everyone has a mind that is like a garden. Plant seeds of positive thought everywhere you go. Look for the good in every situation. I believe that every day that I am lucky enough to be here to help others, is a successful day.

My greatest personal success is realizing what empowers me, and knowing what I am capable of accomplishing. I still have so much more to do and I believe that is exactly why I was cured of my diagnosis in 2006.

———————

Natasha Duswalt is a published author, speaker, and the president and founder of Peak Models & Talent in Los Angeles.

As an international model, Natasha had the rare opportunity to travel all over the world in places including New York, Miami, Hong Kong, Japan, Taiwan, Mexico and several other locations working with top designers and companies.

Peak Models & Talent has been touted as one of Los Angeles' top agencies, booking with high-end clients such as Guess Jeans, Manhattan Beachwear, Intel, Nokia, Reebok, Disney, ABS Clothing, Speedo, Tempurpedic Sleep Systems, Starbucks, Nissan, Cialis, Wells Fargo, Honda, Patagonia, Princess Cruises, Tommy Bahama, Kmart and Target just to name a few.

In October of 2006 Natasha was diagnosed with Hodgkin's Lymphoma cancer. Natasha's inspirational message reminds us what is possible and what we are capable of achieving. There is no limit once you realize that you are here for a limited time, and you were born with everything you need.

Natasha currently lives in Los Angeles with her husband Craig and their three children.

www.PeakModels.com

Man of Steel

by Dean Cain

I 'm 8 years old and playing in my first-ever organized basketball game. The kid guarding me is much quicker—everywhere I turn, he's already there, like an annoying gnat. Finally, I grab him by the shirt and throw him to the ground. Whistles blow and parents complain. My dad turns to my mom and says, "Maybe he should play football."

For the next 14 years, my mettle was hammered-out on the gridiron. I didn't have time or interest in drugs or other distractions, because I was too focused. Football helped me get into Princeton University, where I became an All-American and briefly made it to the NFL with the Buffalo Bills (knee injury…a different book). Football helped me make friends, because having 110 teammates ensures plenty of diversity and challenges and close interaction. Football helped me vent and channel frustration and aggression and anger into hard work, discipline, and ultimately, success.

I love athletics. They tell you so much about a person's character. What kind of teammate are you? How do you react to adversity? Are you coachable? How do you respond when you're tired, or sick, or injured, or under tremendous pressure? How do you react to a bad call? This is not to say that people HAVE to play sports (my own son doesn't play team sports—he trains in mixed martial arts), but athletics were essential to my overall development.

I love competition. Growing up, I played every sport under the sun. Four and five sports a year, all year 'round for 15 years. I learned how to win. I learned how to lose. I learned how to get back up after being knocked down. I learned that everyone gets knocked down. Everyone. I was voted top athlete in my high school. I was voted top athlete at my college. I lettered in 3 different sports at Princeton, but no sport could hold a candle to my love for football.

I love contact. In high school, my football/track coach said, "Cain, you're the only guy I know who runs FASTER when he HITS the hurdles!" In college, I ran my 40-yard-dash faster with my gear on. Running without my helmet and shoulder pads felt awkward, like a knight without his armor. Football was a great fit for me, but the road to RockStar success is never easy.

I wanted to kill my college football coach. Literally. Before my sophomore year at Princeton, the head coach was fired. Under the new regime, I tried to switch from defensive back to receiver but was quickly sent back to the defense. They never had any intention of letting me play offense. My new defensive back coach was called, "Vermin." That wasn't his real name, but that's what a few of us called him. It was not a term of endearment.

As the only sophomore starting on the defense, and starting at cornerback, Vermin let me know that opposing teams would be targeting me. He let me know this every day, every practice, every meeting. He would scream at me all day long, until his voice went hoarse (which I took as a small victory). Vermin drove me and drove me and yelled at me—right in my face, EVERY SINGLE DAY. I took to staring defiantly into his beady little eyes, silent, and stone-faced. Vermin wouldn't let me drop a single ball in practice. EVER. Every pass in the air he expected me to intercept. Every tackle he expected me to make. This dude was all over me. As the season wound down, I was considering leaving Princeton and taking one of the many scholarships that had been offered to me out of high school (the Ivy League does NOT give athletic scholarships).

My dad flew to Princeton from the jungles of Brazil to catch the final game of my sophomore season. Dad had been directing a film for 6 months in the middle of the Amazon, had grown a jungle beard, and contracted malaria (he hadn't realized that yet). He didn't have time to go home to see my mother or the rest of the family in California. He had missed all my games (there was no Internet back then), and he wasn't gonna miss this last one. I talked with my tanned, skinny, and bearded dad about Vermin and all the crap he had put me through. Dad patiently gave me some sage farm-boy advice (he was raised on a farm in South Dakota). Then he told me to finish up the season and the semester, and afterward we'd discuss transferring to another school if I still wished.

We played Cornell the next day, and I faced-off with their stud All-Ivy receiver. He was big and strong, and supposed to dominate me. We had a war all afternoon, and with time winding down they were driving for the winning score. They threw to the stud, but I stepped in front and picked it off for the <u>third</u> time of the day! I weaved my way through defenders and stepped out of bounds, sealing the victory! My teammates hoisted me onto their shoulders. RockStar!

I stayed at Princeton and continued to excel at defensive back. Junior year I was moved to free safety, where I really belonged. Vermin continued to ride me like a donkey, but I was getting tougher. The team had a terrible year, but I had another great season. The individual recognition felt hollow because the team hadn't won. As my senior season was about to begin, our beloved head coach suffered a heart attack and died. It was a devastating loss.

My family decided to move to Princeton for my senior season. They went to every single game, home and away. My father had just gotten his biggest break in Hollywood and was preparing to direct the film *Young Guns*. He was traveling back to Los Angeles during the week and then returning to Princeton for the weekend games. It was awesome to have their support. I was having the greatest season any defensive back had ever had in college football, and Vermin and I had made peace. I realized Vermin was like the character "Fletcher" that J. K. Simmons had won an Academy Award for playing in the film *Whiplash*. Vermin had driven me that hard to make me great. (Today we are still great friends, and Vermin continues to coach football at Princeton.)

The final game of my college career was at Princeton. Cornell again. My entire family was there. My girlfriend was there. It was the coldest game anyone could remember. With the wind-chill factor, it was -20 Fahrenheit. My sister still complains that it permanently screwed-up the circulation in her feet (they were blue, and a woman had to put them inside her fur coat). At the end of the first half, I intercept my 10th pass of the season to leave me one interception shy of the single-season NCAA record (11). In the third quarter, a pass bounces off the chest of a Cornell receiver and directly into my hands! I've tied the record! I run it back, get knocked out of bounds on our sideline, and promptly make my way over to the stands. I toss the ball to my father. He throws it back. I throw it back harder and tell him, "That's for <u>you</u>!"

That moment is still my all-time favorite sports highlight. After all the blood, sweat, tears, fights with Vermin, and separation from my family, I got to tie the NCAA record and throw that football to my dad in the stands. I was finally a friggin' RockStar!

Later in the game, I intercepted another pass, and broke the NCAA record for interceptions in a single season and became a SuperRockStar! Two of those NCAA records still stand, and my dad still has his football.

———————

Dean Cain grew up in Malibu, CA, and has appeared in over 100 films, including *Out Of Time*, opposite Denzel Washington, *God's Not Dead, The Broken Hearts Club, Vendetta*, and the soon-to-be-released *Gosnell*. Dean has also starred in dozens of television films and series and is perhaps best known for his role as Superman on ABC's *Lois & Clark*. Dean also hosted and produced the long-running series *Ripley's Believe It Or Not*. Known for his incredible work ethic, Dean is currently starring in a wide array of projects, including the third season of VH1's hit series *Hit the Floor*, recurring on the widely popular CBS series *Supergirl*, and hosting the third season of the CW smash *Masters of Illusion*. An accomplished screenwriter, in 2015 Dean penned four separate feature films, three of which are slated to begin production in 2016. An athlete at heart, Dean attended Princeton University, and was an All-American defensive back, setting two NCAA records for interceptions. He signed with the Buffalo Bills, but a knee injury quickly ended his professional sports career before it had begun.

Twitter: @RealDeanCain

RELAX!

by Glenn Morshower

Here's a great business tip on how to relax.

I'm sure you've had the experience of going to a meeting or to a job interview. And the finest version of that job interview was the one that happened in the car on the way home after the actual meeting. Have you ever been there? You go through the implications, the woulda, coulda, shoulda's, and you're wishing, "if only I had done it differently"— but you didn't. You're wondering why your hands were quivering, why they were sweaty. And your normal voice went into a higher register. Everything went wrong.

The bottom line is you were too nervous to relax and really share with them who it is you are.

Years ago I got a handle on this—it was really a gift from the heavens. I was scheduled to read for my first television series regular role, I was headed out the door, and I got one of those "whispers." I turned around, went back inside, and my wife, Carolyn, said, "Is everything all right, did you forget something?" I said, "No, I just got a whisper." She said, "What did you hear?" She knows about me and my whispers. I said, "I just was told that I need to go to ABC with my shoes full of syrup." Yes, maple syrup, and full too, not a couple drops.

We filled my shoes with maple syrup, and I've never felt more relaxed in my life. I literally arrived to the television network, squishing, and it was my beautiful secret. I'm standing there, a full-grown man, in syrup, and nobody knows. I watched when the waft of the syrup hit them, and watched them looking at each other thinking, "Why does it all of a sudden smell like the International House of Pancakes in here?" They would never dream it's coming from the actor. I mean, who walks around smelling like maple syrup?

And because I was relaxed, I got the job. It was a series regular role, and it was more money than I had ever earned at the time. We did the pilot, and a few weeks later I went on another interview. I did it again, and again I had never been more relaxed, and again I booked the job. This went on six straight times with six straight hires, every one of them with various items in my shoes. I added honey to the mix, and at one point, I think it was job number four, I put little baby marshmallows in between my toes.

Do this. Don't judge it, just do it. Go back to being a kid.

I kept booking jobs and started wondering, if it worked that well in my shoes, I wonder where else I might want to place things.

I wanted to do something really different for my meeting to book the job as a series regular on the hit television series, "24." So, I walked into the meeting with Oscar Meyer bologna folded in half and inserted right between my butt cheeks. I did. For those of you who are taking life too seriously, there is nothing that will repair your seriousness quicker than bologna between your butt cheeks.

I walked in, and if you think you get relaxed and not caring about anything when your shoes are full of syrup, trust me, when you've got bologna in-between your butt cheeks, it's impossible to have a bad day.

That's my secret.

One of my acting students tried this. He called me and said, "I am zero for ninety. Ninety interviews and not even one call back. I was getting ready to pack up and leave Los Angeles, but I went to your seminar tonight, and I'm thinking maybe food in the undershorts could be what I've been missing. I don't know if I should do it, though—it feels a little risky."

"Risky" is the word he used. I said, "What exactly is your level of risk when you are zero for ninety?"

So he tried it. He took the challenge, and a week later he called me, and his voice was quivering. I thought, "Oh son of a gun, he did it. I know he did it."

And he did. He said, "Glenn, I uh…"

I interrupted and said, "Did you do the food in the undershorts thing?"
He said, "I did, and I got my very first call back. I have taken Meisner training, transcendental meditation, I have four 10-minute Shakespearean monologues memorized, and none of them made a difference. Then I went and I put food in my undershorts and I got my first call back."

I said, "Well all right, that's good."

He said, "That's not the end of the story. They called me about ten minutes ago and told me I booked the job. I just got my very first job."

I said, "Very proud my friend, but there's one missing piece to the story. What did you do?"

He said, "Do you promise you won't judge me?"

I said, "Buddy, I booked a series with Eric Roberts wearing a bra. Not one that they saw, but I was wearing one. My wife helped me put it on. It was under my suit, and I was playing the head of the FBI and had a bra on." I continued, "So, what did you do?"

He said, "I took an entire handful of Kellogg's Frosted Flakes, mashed them up, and wedged them right up between my butt cheeks. Have you ever done that?"

I said, "No, no… I've never done that."

He said, "Well what do you think?"

I couldn't resist because I'm an improv teacher. I said, "Are you kidding me? Kellogg's Frosted Flakes? I think that's GRRRRREAT."

One of the busiest character actors in Hollywood today, Glenn Morshower has appeared in over 200 films and television shows, in a career spanning four decades. Audiences worldwide know Glenn best for his seven-year run as Agent Aaron Pierce, on the FOX hit series 24. Glenn currently appears as Wayne Lowry, on the Netflix original series Bloodline, and as General Sam Lane, on the new CBS series Supergirl. Glenn recently produced, and starred in his first independent feature film, *Flutter*, which is currently available on Hulu, iTunes and Amazon. When Glenn is not busy filming, he travels extensively as a motivational speaker with his program, *The Extra Mile*. He has spoken to audiences all over the world.

www.GlennMorshower.com

FIVE DAYS

by Ernie Hudson

I n the fall of 1961, I was 15 years old and starting my first year in senior
high school. I didn't have many friends. I lived in the projects with
my brother and grandmother, who took us in after my mother died of
tuberculosis. I never knew my dad, so Mama was all there was.

I knew we were poor, but I never imagined we were "Poor" poor. There
were so many people around less fortunate than we were. Mama was someone
people turned to when they were in trouble. We canned fruit to store up for
the winter but ran out early because we gave most of it to people in need.
People called her Ma. "One thing for certain," she'd say, "they are all God's
children. Who am I to turn away one of God's own?"

I had never really gone without eating. That fall I noticed food was not
being replenished. I sat at the kitchen table staring at a pot of rice. I was angry.
We'd had rice for three days straight. Where was the rest of the food? She said
things were tight right now. I shouted they wouldn't be if she'd stop giving
all of our food away. She calmly explained it was five days before her check
came, and we were out of money. She had been counting on getting paid, but
they wouldn't have the money for another week. She planned go to our pastor
and ask for a small loan until her check came. She cleaned the church every
Saturday, usually by herself, and seldom got so much as a thank you. She was
the one they called when they couldn't find anyone else to serve.

That night at church, when she came out of the pastor's office, I knew he had said no. Just before the closing prayers, the pastor's wife announced that me and Mama had no money or food to eat. She begged people to take up an offering for us. I was mortified. I was tempted to scream, shut up! But I knew that would only make things worse. They raised two dollars and fourteen cents. No amount of money was worth the humiliation I felt.

That night we shared a bag of Lipton tea and some Saltine crackers. Mama was trying to put on a brave face, but I could feel her sense of defeat. We sat in silence until I picked up a cracker and asked, "How many people could Jesus feed with one Saltine cracker?" We both started laughing. When we finally stopped, there was a quiet peace that filled the room. She looked at me with a love so deep that it brings tears to my eyes even to this day.

That night while lying in bed, I wondered if I could last five days without eating. At church the adults would have day-long fasts, but never five days. I made up my mind to do it. Jesus fasted for 40 days, so I asked God to please help me make it for just five days.

DAY 1

I woke up hungry. School was a three-mile walk, and the weather had turned cold. At school, word had gotten around that I was poor and starving. It upset me, but I was too tired to fight. At lunch I pretended to study so I'd be left alone. When I got home from school, Mama had prepared dinner, but I refused to eat. "You have to eat." Mama said, "If you don't eat, you're going to get sick, and we don't have money to take you to the doctor." I told her that God had told me to fast. She finally said, "Okay, but if you're not going to eat, I'm not going to eat either." She made me promise that if I started to get sick or too hungry and tired, we would break the fast.

DAY 2

We started the day with a prayer, but it kept getting interrupted by my stomach growling. At school, it was hard to focus, and the walk home that day was freezing. Secretly I was hoping that Mama had gone ahead and prepared dinner. Instead, she anointed my head with oil and we prayed.

DAY 3

I was exhausted and lacked concentration, but I was getting through the day until gym class. I tried to opt out by saying I wasn't feeling well, but the gym instructor wasn't buying it. "Suit up!" I panicked. What if I passed out on the basketball court? Our high school was State Basketball Champions. How was I going to make it through this practice? I closed my eyes, took a moment to quiet my mind, and flashed back to the night Mama and I sat at the table laughing. I could hear her warm laughter. The feeling of peace that I felt that night took over my body, and somehow I let go of everything, including the hunger. When I entered the game, I was focused and feeling surprisingly strong. I didn't just play, I dominated the game. What had just happened? It didn't take long for the hunger and exhaustion to return, yet somehow I was aware of the hunger but in a different way. I told Mama what had happened. She said Peter walked on water just like Jesus. As long as he kept his eyes on Christ he was fine, but when he turned his attention to the storm that was raging, he went under. "Keep your focus on your peace within," she said.

DAY 4

On day four I became aware of when I was in that quiet place and when I was not. I realized I was making a choice, although not always a consciously. For the first time, I understood the Bible verse about waiting on the Lord to renew your strength.

DAY 5

On the fifth day, my laughter returned. That night we attended church. I sat with Mama, smiling, knowing we were sharing something truly special. On our walk home from church Mama stared up at the night sky and said everything was held together by the power of God. It was the same power that had created me and everyone else. It is always available to us if we just remember to use it.

The next day, Mama made a big pot of vegetable soup. To this day, it was the best soup I've ever had.

It's now been over fifty years. Since then I've made it a point to fast at least once a year. Sometimes just a few days and sometimes longer. I don't do it for religious reasons; I like the discipline and the idea of turning away from the constant desire for food. Before Mama made her transition, I told her that those five days were one of the best learning experiences I'd ever had. The lessons weren't just about food—they apply to all the fears and challenges life throws our way. I can choose what I focus on. There is a place within me that I can go to and find strength regardless of circumstance, and if I listen carefully, I can hear Mama's laughter, and it never fails to make me smile.

———————

Ernie Hudson is one of the most sought-after actors of our time, with an impressive list of credits and awards and whose body of work has diverse range. Hudson joined Bill Murray, Dan Akroyd, and Harold Ramis in the 1984 feature film *Ghostbusters* and in the sequel, *Ghostbusters 2,* and recently filmed a pivotal cameo in *Ghostbusters 3*. Hudson's films include *The Hand that Rocks the Cradle, Congo,* and *The Crow,* among many others. Television appearances include *Oz, Law & Order, Modern Family, Grey's Anatomy, Criminal Minds,* and *Key and Peele.* He currently co-stars in Netflix's hot series *Grace & Frankie* opposite Lily Tomlin and Jane Fonda and is shooting *Graves* in which he stars opposite Nick Nolte and Sela Ward.

www.ErnieHudsonOfficial.com

TENACITY

by Larry Broughton

S
uck it up and drive on" was my mantra that cold evening in the rural hills of North Carolina—I couldn't let myself give up. I'd spent the day scrounging for edible plants, bugs, and small animals but only came up with a couple of plump worms and a lone grasshopper for nourishment. Anything I could have eaten had either fled or been destroyed by the fire.

In order to complete this phase of my journey to become one the military's elite Green Berets, the cadre of the US Army's Special Forces Qualification Course had dropped me off in an area that was to be my home for the next few days. It was my lame luck the forest service had conducted a controlled burn of the area just weeks before, clearing the tall grass and underbrush small animals usually used for shelter. The course requirements were to build some sort of shelter and fire, with a laundry list of improvised tools and traps that made my inner-Eagle Scout want to run home, crying to mamma. The fire that had charred and stripped the area of fuel and food made my tasks nearly impossible.

The original class of a couple hundred wannabe Green Berets had been thinned out during the weeks leading up to the survival phase. Most who left the program were VWs (Voluntary Withdraws) or, as we simply called them, "quitters." They simply lacked the mental and physical toughness to meet the challenges that were thrown at us. For weeks we'd been running on one small meal a day while stretching our brains with instructional classes, assessing our

27

physical capabilities with long runs and forced marches through the North Carolina sun and sands, and testing our intestinal fortitude by pushing the limits of our warrior spirit.

The added stress of carrying weapons and full rucksacks on the marches made many candidates pass-out due to heat exhaustion or dehydration. We endured training sessions and log-drills in the muddy hand-to-hand combatives pit at 2 a.m., excruciating obstacle courses that made some men cry from pain or fear, and leadership and team building exercises that were meant to test our capabilities during high-stress situations in combat conditions. No matter what was going on around me though, no matter how many people were throwing-up, passing out, or quitting, I kept repeating to myself, "Just take one more step. Just put one dusty boot in front of the other."

It was unseasonably cold that night. I huddled to the warmth and glow of my small fire (built dangerously close to my thatched lean-to hooch), "enjoying" my two fried worms (that were supposed to taste like bacon—they lied), and my grasshopper. I sipped my hot pine needle tea while peering down at one of the small "tools" we were issued just moments before we were dropped in the forest. It was a book of matches from the popular Winn Dixie grocery store chain found throughout the South. On the front cover was a picture of the most beautiful steak I had ever seen, and on the back cover was smiling pig that looked right at me. I was certain the Cadre distributed these particular matches less as a tool to start a fire (after all, we knew how to do that without matches) and more as a mind-game to toy with us during this starvation survival phase of the course.

As I sat there staring into my small fire, a soft rain started to fall. In the distance I heard a muffled "pop," so I stumbled to my feet. A split second later, I saw the light of an aerial flare from one of my fellow candidates. As the brilliant colors lit up the sky, I thought to myself, "quitter." We were issued a flare to deploy in the event we were injured and needed assistance, or if we were ready to VW. I was certain this was a VW, and it meant one less guy I had to compete with.

Light-headed and dizzy, due to the quick movement and the lack of food, I leaned against a tree and watched the light from the flare dissipate and listened to the sound of the rain. A couple minutes later I heard another "pop." As the pace of the rain increased, so did the number of flares lighting the sky around me. I sat shivering in my hooch, listening to the rain, dreaming of hot chocolate and warm dry sheets.

How many people quit on something, just short of their goal, not knowing success is right around the corner? I've seen countless early quitters in my life who've thrown in the towel the *first time* they failed at something, or when the going got tough. I tend not to have much sympathy for those early quitters. However, my heart breaks most for those who've dug deep inside through difficult times, persevered over and over again, and given up just short of the prize.

My wrestling coach used to bark, "Winners NEVER quit, and quitters never win!" The simple reason some winners never quit is because they'd hate to wake up and realize just one more push could have driven them past their goal. Additionally, they've recognized that failure is a natural part of succeeding; and if they're not failing, then they're not moving fasting enough or getting close enough to their fullest potential.

We must accept that adverse market conditions, competitors, and our own missteps will always seem to get in the way of immediately attaining our goals. Here's the truth: The single most important ingredient, tool, or technique that will ensure enduring success has been a critical piece of the victory equation in arts, industry, politics, and sports for centuries. In a word, it's "TENACITY."

Nothing will serve us better on our journey towards success and significance than the combination of learning from our failures and maintaining a tenacious spirit—simply digging deep, moving forward, outlasting our competition, and hanging on while others let go. Talent, education, and genius, without action and perseverance, will never be a match for the tenacious, never-surrender attitude.

Success requires grit, effort, and hard work. Most folks don't want to commit to that, and so they simply don't succeed (if, that is, they even have the guts to try). Don't focus on them; focus on those who have shown success over and over again. Examine them; exam their technique; examine their team; but most of all, examine their attitude and philosophy on success and failure. After all, success leaves clues.

If you find yourself longing for the "good life," or you feel resentment or jealousy towards those who are living their dreams, it's time to take a look in the mirror. Have you honestly been tenacious in the pursuit of your dreams?

How long have you been reaching for that prize? How hard have you really worked for it? You must understand this: Most high-achievers have sacrificed big time, they manage their shortcomings, they are dogged in their approach, and they want success as much as a drowning man wants air to breathe. More than any other ingredient, the key to overcoming failure and realizing enduring success is TENACITY.

Larry Broughton is Founder/CEO of broughtonHOTELS.com and BROUGHTONadvisory.com as well as yoogozi.com, an exciting website offering bite-size nuggets of learning for leaders and high achievers. He's a best-selling author, a keynote speaker, an award-winning entrepreneur & CEO, and a former US Army Green Beret. He is a regular expert commentator on topics relating to leadership and entrepreneurship on MSNBC, the Travel Channel's Hotel Impossible, CNBC, and dozens of network news programs around the country.

www.LarryBroughton.me

LETTING GO—A LIFE PHD FROM MISTAKES UNIVERSITY

by Nick Lowery

I n 1990, I had my best scoring year in the NFL—hell, I led the NFL in scoring, and received not only the NFL All Pro team but Pro Football Weekly's "Golden Toe" award as the best kicker OR punter in the NFL! Can't get much better than that! The second most field goals in a season in NFL history, the Kansas City Chiefs record for points in a season, 24 field goals in a row into the playoffs...really good stuff...especially after following my worst season ever. Even though I was already the most accurate kicker in NFL history at the time, I had been humiliated in one intense, dark, insane, very cold, and very public 15-minute span of time the year before on a muddy, frigid field in the old Cleveland Stadium.

That taught me once again that we must always cherish the hunger for greatness, the urgency, the humility to love the awkward, uneven process of **hard work** that is at its core. As I look back, I used that profoundly painful event—3 missed field goals right at the end of the game and overtime, to *re-learn* what I already knew deep in my bones: that it's all about pulling out the stops, devoting yourself to and totally **trusting** your preparation as **the only way** to allow yourself to find a new level. I made a conscious decision to **let go** of both the expectations and judgments of others, and many of my own as well. I gave back to myself that simple power to be the best I could be, to

31

be content to focus only on perfecting God's beautiful gifts to me. That's all we can ever do! Find that peace to bring all our energy, all our focus, all our discipline and passion to our own four-by-three-yard-square *office* between the hash marks on the field. For me, that lonely Persian rug shaped, Magic Carpet ride to complete fear and totally insane *life-giving* risk.

I knew that the standards and goals that I had set for my performance exceeded the expectations of others, and that was enough. How sad to live a life where not only do we never taste the best we can be, but we live based on the standards, judgments, and expectations *of others*. In essence, we are living someone else's life! To me, it's only the conversation with ourselves and God's purpose waiting to be awakened and set on fire that is where the Light truly lives.

We all have and will have defeats and losses. We all will make a thousand mistakes along the way. I say, make a million mistakes—try so many times that the fear of mistakes becomes the brilliant enlightenment and confirmation that making unlimited mistakes is giving permission to be ONESELF.

The New England Patriots were undefeated through the entire season and into the Super Bowl a few years ago, yet in the end they ended with a crushing loss that interrupted and destroyed their dream of a perfect season. That year may be more painful than many less outstanding ones, because sometimes in the midst of great effort and extraordinary achievement, **failure still rears its head**. But Failure is merely Greatness and Wisdom in disguise.

We all have bad, even horrible games. We will all miss our own field goals, sometimes even the potential game-winners. We fall short of our own expectations; but at least they are our own! How much better to focus the expectations at superb **preparation**? How about not worrying about the outcome? The great players stay focused on the work at hand, and find a way to remain alert yet relaxed as the process of their own form of field goal and scoring points unfolds. They find peace knowing they have done the good work to be ready for the chaos of life and the game…and trust that preparation as they enter the fire, because that practice was likely as hard or harder than the game.

With minutes left in the 1988 Super Bowl, down 16–13, millions worldwide watching, Joe Montana famously looks at the 10 faces staring back at him in the huddle. His steely eyes scan what looks to be the sideline…and then he turns to tackle Harris Barton and calmly says, "Hey, look up there in the stands next to the exit ramp, *isn't that John Candy*?!" And then leads the 49ers methodically 92 yards down the field, looking off his favorite receiver, Jerry Rice, and oh so calmly throwing the winning touchdown to John Taylor with 34 seconds left.

Leaders (and truly great players are always leaders in their own way) leave the history writers to the analysis and the verbal pieces of the story—*his-story*—so to speak, to others and afterwards. Hell, today the writers and fans Tweet DURING the game! They try to predict the heroes *before* the script is even written. Today's players—and you and I—must shrug off the enormous temptation to focus on the outcome before the outcome is achieved!

The media tries to **bully** a player's attention away from the right things and turn a Tom Brady, Drew Brees, Aaron Rodgers, Cam Newton, and RG3 into Hall of Famers in one season...or even 7 games...or, they trash them into complete failures just as fast! All NFL greats like Tom Brady, Brett Farve, Johnny Unitas, and Joe Montana have tasted defeat. Some knuckle-head will always criticize our performance. Think about it! The better we are, the more people are watching...the more visible and interesting we are...and the more expectations and people to please...or to **ignore.**

So how can we focus when so many cameras become a collective mirror that blocks the sense of space, distance, and context we all prefer? If we spend our minutes, hours, or days worrying about the expectations of others, we miss out on what is happening **now**! And being present in THIS MOMENT, my friends, is the essence of living and winning! Those moments of being fully, calmly, charismatically alive to ourselves and others; alive to each breath we take; each pair of eyes we connect with—equally alive to the unique energy, spirit, and story that people bring to **us**. A moment of truth is not just the apex moments, it is also a presentness truly full when it is about the little details, small surprises, and miracles of our whole world, not just us!

The *narcissistic hero athlete kicker* in us (speaking from experience!) sometimes takes much too long to learn. The universe is unlimited and infinite in value. It's our choice to invest in the currency of success and not that of defeat. More than the traditional idea of success, I am talking—no I am singing—about a tactile feeling far beyond any naive notions of intuition. It's that feeling that takes place in our heart's epicenter, where instead of seeing ourselves as impostors and saboteurs in our own defeats and re-affirmed failures, we brand ourselves *legitimate* and *worthy* and *loved*. **And that, my friends—is victory!**

Nick Lowery transcends any category. Hall of Famer, Ivy League scholar, presidential aide, author and poet, teacher, and philanthropist. The Kansas City Chiefs Hall of Famer was the most accurate kicker in NFL History. Nick's story is about **persistence that leads to Focus, Passion, and Purpose.** Nick won the NFL Man of the Year award for both the Kansas City Chiefs and New York Jets. The Harvard and Dartmouth graduate is the winner of the NFL Player's humanitarian award, the **Byron Whizzer White award**. For information about Nick's speaking or community work, contact Nick at **Nick@Loweryspeaks.com** or visit...

www.nicklowery.org

FROM PASSION TO ACQUISITION: A $20 MILLION ROCK STAR BY 30!

by Nellie Akalp

I think we're all entitled to have a "Rock Star" moment at some point in our lives. I'm fortunate to have had a pretty amazing one: selling my first business for $20 million in my early thirties!

But my story began far before that...

After my family migrated to the US from Iran in 1976, my grandparents dove right into that American Dream and started an antique business selling Persian antiques.

As a child, I noted the responsibilities (vision, determination, and passion!) that my family had in running their own business. They struggled; it wasn't easy running a business in a new country. But they loved what they did, and that stuck with me. I saw how much they were willing to sacrifice for this business.

I may have been too young to help out at the antique shop, but I still grew up thinking that starting and running a business was the norm. As I got older, my grandparents put me to work at the subsequent businesses they opened, first at their Mediterranean restaurant and later at their Swenson's Ice Cream franchise.

I didn't graduate high school ready to take on the family business or even start my own business. In fact, I thought I wanted to be a lawyer. Chalk it up to watching too many television programs like Law and Order that made law look glamorous and fun. But once I got to law school, I realized it wasn't what I wanted to do for the rest of my life.

In 1997, my husband, Phil (who I'd met in college), was struggling in his corporations class (which is ironic, as you'll soon see), and he felt immersing himself in the subject would allow him to bring his grade up. What better way to do that than to start a business helping companies incorporate online? I was immediately on board.

We took $100 and set up a website, and our first company, MyCorporation. com, was born in December 1997. Then, Phil started publishing content on our teeny one-page website, and, before we knew it, we had our first client wanting to form an Oregon corporation. We didn't have employees. Heck, we didn't even have an office; we operated out of our two-bedroom apartment, and that was all we needed.

Our little two-person business filing company took off, to our surprise, and after graduating with my Juris Doctor degree in 1998, I decided to quit my law job so that I could focus wholeheartedly on building our business.

Despite not having formal training in running a business beyond watching my family of entrepreneurs, I inherently had a knack for it. I knew that when the client called, we had to go out of our way, listen to their needs, and provide a solution based on what they needed—under promise and over deliver. It was so easy to gain Internet traffic back then that we were just trying to keep up with the influx of orders. The business was growing faster than we could keep up with it.

As we grew the business, it got the attention of Intuit in 2005, who offered us $20 million for the company. When we sold the company, we felt like absolute Rock Stars because, in addition to us, there were a few other well-known competitors in the industry that were being considered for acquisition as well, and we were the chosen one and were named the "Pioneers of the Legal document filing industry." We never could have dreamed of the successes we had achieved in such a short time…so it was definitely a "Rock Star" moment for us.

After staying on as advisors for a while, we realized that the business had lost its entrepreneurial spirit for us to stay on and hence took off to enjoy time with our family; but that didn't last long, and I felt like I was crawling out of my skin. I did everything I ever wanted to do, from considering opening up a boutique cardio fitness facility; I even started a clothing business selling custom hand-painted tie dye clothing out of the trunk of my Mercedes S550, but I felt unfulfilled and unsatisfied and was ready to get back to work—my heart and passion still remained in small business.

And so once our non-compete clause expired in 2009, my husband Phil and I got back into the business filing game. We realized how passionate and determined we were about helping people find their entrepreneurial dream and turning it into a business, and so, in 2009, we launched our current business, CorpNet.com.

This time around, we were providing the same services we had with our first company, but we were finding it much harder to compete in what was now a crowded marketplace. We'd done virtually no marketing or advertising the first go 'round (we hadn't needed to), and now with the rise in popularity of Internet marketing, I had no clue where to begin.

Fortunately, I'm a tenacious person, so I quickly taught myself how to establish CorpNet and myself as small business experts within the industry. I devoured blogs, books, seminars, classes, and everything else I could get my hands on to learn how to win big in this new landscape in the face of having so many eyes on me, this being my second time around in the same industry.

I knew CorpNet was going to be a success when I increased our pricing and saw our volume increase. That was a validation of the fact that our clients were coming to us—not because of our competitive pricing—but for our service and what we stood for in the business community: making business dreams into a reality with personal, professional, and timely service.

CorpNet has become more successful than we could have ever imagined. In 2015, CorpNet was recognized on the Inc. 5000 list as one of the fastest-growing privately held companies in America, with a 149% growth rate in three years. And as my wonderful team helps me manage its growth, I have turned my attention towards helping other entrepreneurs successfully find their passion and start, run, and grow their businesses successfully.

Today, I am internationally recognized as one of the most prominent experts on small business legal matters, contributing my content regularly to media outlets such as Business Insider, Small Business Trends, Entrepreneur, Forbes, Mashable, The Wall Street Journal, The Huffington Post, and a dozen other sites and blogs that are dedicated to small business. I've also shared my business advice on television and radio programs such as FOX Small

Business, FOX 5 in Las Vegas, and Small Business Trends Radio. Each month, my regular columns and small business advice reach more than eight million people nationwide.

I may have felt like a Rock Star when Intuit bought our first business, but I've continued to feel like a Rock Star every day since, because I'm doing exactly what I want to do—which is inspiring, motivating, and helping other entrepreneurs realize what their business passion is and helping them bring it to life and thriving at it.

———————

Nellie Akalp is an entrepreneur, small business expert, speaker, and mother of four amazing kids. As CEO of CorpNet.com, she has helped more than half a million entrepreneurs launch their businesses. Akalp is nationally recognized as one of the most prominent experts on small business legal matters, contributing frequently to outlets like Entrepreneur, Forbes, The Huffington Post, Mashable, and Fox Small Business. A passionate entrepreneur herself, Akalp is committed to helping others take the reins and dive into small business ownership. Through her public speaking, media appearances, and frequent blogging, she has developed a strong following within the small business community and has been honored as a Small Business Influencer Champion three years in a row.

www.Corpnet.com

As Seen on TV! Crash, Burn, Transcend!

by Darren Kavinoky

I didn't appear to be headed towards "rock star success." Partying like a rock star? Sure! Trashing hotel rooms like a rock star? Absolutely! But success? Not so much.

As a kid, I always felt like I was on the outside looking in, like everyone else had an owner's manual to life, and I was absent when they were given out. It didn't help that I was a fat kid, uncomfortable in my own skin. I vividly recall wearing jeans from Sears called "Toughskins." Worse, my Toughskins came in a size called "husky." They should have called them "loser fat-kid jeans" instead; I knew exactly what "husky" *really* meant.

Worse, because of my mom's remarriage(s), we relocated from California to Oregon to Virginia, where we lived on the outskirts of a very affluent area. (When I say "outskirts," I mean a crappy apartment that just happened to be near the brick-and-white-column mansions my schoolmates lived in.) The kids I was surrounded by navigated life with a seeming ease that I lacked. They didn't wear anything "husky" sized. They wore boating shoes and shirts with little alligators. They did things that seemed impossible to me, like going to class, studying Latin, and doing homework.

As a 12-year-old, I was assigned the school project of writing a career report. The cover page of that report hangs in my office today. The overly-neat cursive writing of a junior high school student reads

This is a story of what I, Darren Kavinoky, will be like ten years from now. Or, rather, a speculation of what I will be like ten years from now. I feel that while a person's physical features may change, their basic psyche stays the same. If my philosophy holds true, I will probably be a bum. Or even worse, a lawyer. *Either way, you end up drinking something out of a brown paper bag. The only difference is where.*

Oddly prophetic, since at that time I hadn't consumed anything that was mind- or mood-altering (other than junk food!), but clearly I needed something.

All of that changed just one year later. I was now a 13-year-old, still wearing husky-sized Toughskins, but I found myself at a party that I had no business being at, since all the "cool kids" were there. A small cluster of the really cool guys were passing around a joint; one of them passed it my way. I wish I could tell you that I had a crisis of conscience or any form of "Just say no!" in that moment. But that would be a lie. Because if you felt about yourself like I felt about myself, and one of the cool kids offered you a joint, there was nothing to do but take it.

In that one moment, everything changed. In that one moment, I no longer felt like I was on the outside looking in. I could now hang with the cool guys and tell some jokes and they'd laugh. I could now talk to the pretty girls that I had always wanted to talk to, but couldn't. I no longer felt the button of my husky-sized Toughskins jabbing me in the belly. In that moment, I no longer felt the unbearable weight of just being me.

I remember my 13-year-old brain consciously thinking, "I'm going to feel like *this* every moment from now on." And for the next twenty years I made good on that promise. At first it was fun. Then it was fun, with problems. Then it became nothing but problems.

In my case, that meant ever-declining grades in high school, flunking out of college, getting arrested five different times (in three different countries) for various misbehaviors, all related to my being loaded.

The 90s turned out to be an unpleasant decade for me, as I began to appreciate that I was the common denominator in all of my problems. But by this time, I needed escape like a drowning man needs air, and couldn't stop.

Until another pivotal moment.

I was basically homeless, and my wife (who had thrown me out a couple of years before) was allowing me to stay in her house (what used to be *our* house) only out of the goodness of her heart.

I sat in her study one night, reading a book entitled "The Thinking Person's Guide to Sobriety" (a ridiculous title, since it is our thinking that is so screwed up in the first place, but my ego insisted that no ordinary guide would do; I was nothing if not a deep thinker!). Since I was reading, it only made sense that a joint was burning in the ashtray, and some Crown Royal on the rocks sat close by. As my wife passed by and saw this, she asked "Aren't you supposed to be sober when you read that book?!"

In that one moment, everything changed. Suddenly, I could see myself with a clarity that was new and powerful. In that moment, I knew that if I didn't change, I was a dead man walking. That moment happened on May 9, 2000, and I'm blessed to have lived a radically different lifestyle ever since.

The fat kid in husky-sized Toughskins has now completed seven Ironman triathlons and fits easily into normal sized clothes. The once bankrupt and homeless furniture mover created 1.800.NoCuffs, The Kavinoky Law Firm, a law office that employs dozens of people and does millions of dollars in annual revenue. I now appear on TV as a legal analyst for CNN, NBC's *Today* show, *Entertainment Tonight*, and many other TV and radio programs. I created (and host) my own TV show, *Deadly Sins*, now in its fifth season on Investigation Discovery. I'm privileged speak to audiences all over the world about the possibility of change that resides in all of us and share my recipe for how to accomplish this. The selfish husband whose wife threw him out (deservedly!) has now celebrated twenty years of marriage to that amazing woman. And the best part is that I now have a teenage daughter who has never experienced her daddy under the influence of anything.

If I stand for anything, it is the proposition that if I can do it, you can too. I have achieved some ridiculous, rock star-like success in the face of total disaster. I know that change can happen in a moment. Is this your moment? It sure could be, if you make it your moment. I hope you do!

———

Darren Kavinoky is an award-winning attorney and the creator and host of the hit TV show *Deadly Sins* on Investigation Discovery. He appears as an expert legal and "misbehavior" analyst on dozens of nationally syndicated shows, including the *Today* show, *Dr. Phil*, *Entertainment Tonight*, and many more. As a keynote speaker, Darren carries a message of hope to audiences worldwide.

www.DarrenKavinoky.com

HOW I PASSED THE MOST CRUCIAL TEST OF MY CAREER

by Hepsharat Amadi, M.D.

I tell my children to always be open to learning, because you never know when the knowledge you attain might become crucial, or when Life will spring a test on you!

I am a conventionally trained family practice doctor who always understood that conventional medicine, while working well for emergencies, was not capable of helping an already healthy person become any healthier.

So I understood, before going to medical school, that my purpose in going there was just to lay the foundation for my medical knowledge, not to be the sum total of it. Little could I have imagined then that the extra knowledge I was on the path to acquiring would one day save my oldest child's eyesight and health.

My aspirations were higher than just managing illness by using drugs and surgery. I wanted to be able to help people get healthy and educated enough to minimize or eliminate their need for medication or emergency services.

That was why, a few years after graduating from S.U.N.Y. at Stony Brook Medical School and completing my residency in Family Practice at Bronx-Lebanon Hospital, I began studying many different holistic health techniques, including earning my license in acupuncture and Chinese herbs at night and on weekends while continuing to work full-time at an outpatient clinic during the day.

My search for more knowledge about how to improve people's health naturally continued, and it was while I was attending yet another health-related seminar that I met a colleague who was also holistically oriented. He introduced me to the quantum biofeedback machine and that really changed my life.

Imagine a machine that consists of a laptop computer, to which a box is attached. The box has leads that can be plugged into it and attach to a patient's head, wrists and ankles, and act as transducers that detect the electromagnetic activity of the entire body. The most familiar analogies I can give you in conventional medicine are the EKG machine for the heart, or the EEG machine for monitoring brain waves.

Now imagine that instead of just printing out squiggly lines that take specialized training to be able to interpret, the quantum biofeedback machine prints out its information in English and numbers! And imagine that instead of only measuring and monitoring the electromagnetic activity of the entire body, the machine can actually also run therapies to improve the way the body functions. How awesome would THAT be?

That is the nature of quantum biofeedback assessment and treatment, and once I saw all the information that could be gleaned from utilizing it, and once I felt the tremendous healing effect it had on me, I was hooked!

I decided I had to have one of these machines to treat myself, my family, and my patients. I was introduced to the quantum biofeedback machine in January of 2003, attended a convention in which I learned more about all the different things it could do in May, and by August of that same year, I had bought my first quantum biofeedback machine and started learning how to use it.

I turned 47 later that year. While I was learning more about using the machine, I had also attended some other seminars about bio-identical hormone replacement and had been doing bio-identical hormone replacement for my patients in my practice.

I began taking bio-identical hormones myself when I was 48. It was the confluence of all these circumstances that allowed me the opportunity to help my oldest daughter, when she was confronted with a major health challenge in January of 2008, five years after I first got the machine.

Around the first week of January, she began complaining of headaches and seeing flashes of blue light. My husband took her to an ophthalmologist

ASAP, who called me to tell me my daughter was having retinal detachment in both eyes and that he was going to refer her to a retinal specialist.

I was shocked, horrified, and very frightened! I knew that retinal detachment, unless treated quickly and well, could lead to permanent blindness.

The retinal specialist she was referred to confirmed this diagnosis after examining her eyes and doing a scan of them called an OCT. In order to treat her retinal detachment, they wanted to put her on a high-dose steroid.

I knew that that could have very bad effects on her in the long run, such as make her gain a lot of weight and weaken her bones and immune system. I was determined to try treating her naturally before I would resort to such a drastic solution as prednisone.

When I began assessing her on the quantum bio-feedback machine, it told me that I "needed to find a glandular solution" to her health problem. So in addition to increasing her nutrition and exercise, I also used the quantum bio-feedback machine not only to treat her but also to find out which bio-identical hormones she needed each day so that I could give them to her.

Within the first two to three weeks of this treatment, her headaches and seeing flashes of blue light stopped, and she began feeling better! I took her back to the retinal specialist several times over the first half of that year so that they could check on her. By the time we made our last visit there, five to six months after this whole crisis had started, they repeated her eye exam and her OCT and they were both absolutely normal, without her ever having used prednisone!

I knew then that I had achieved success and passed a crucial test Life had set for me. I met the challenge of her condition by having enough knowledge to save my daughter's vision and health, naturally.

Hepsharat Amadi, M.D. is a family practice medical doctor who has been providing holistic health care (including quantum biofeedback and bio-identical hormone replacement) in her private practice. She speaks and writes about health and healthcare, and is always interested in learning more.

www.dramadi.com

There Is Nothing Like a Dream to Create the Future—Part One

by Richard Barrier

The very first time I smoked pot was with a good friend. It was 1976, and we went to the movies—we saw "Carrie." While there I thought I heard my parents' voices. I thought, "Great. The first time I get high, and my parents go to the movies. They never go to the movies." I had just started college and was meeting a whole new circle of friends. In high school I was in band and the majority of my friends, my circle of influence, hadn't started college yet.

During these early college days and another "change of associations," I tried everything...with the exception of heroin, peyote, pills, huffing, or main-lining. At one point, for a little too long, I was free-basing cocaine with a blowtorch while starting my first corporate job.

Yes, I am telling you this to shock you and because it is not who I am now. I learned this from Les Brown: Don't beat yourself up for things that you did in the past, because you can't change it, and it's not who you are now. So, you wouldn't do those things now.

In the fall of 1980, I went back to school to California State University at Fullerton. I moved to Fullerton, and in 1982 I got a new corporate job, a really good paying job, new associations, and more money to buy drugs. I had two totally different associations. These associations were as far from East as

45

they were from West, and they never knew each other. I tried to find a balance working with computers at a corporate research facility and with the male dominated Heavy Metal scene. I was a total dichotomy, and I didn't know it. Parts of me were totally split apart from each other. It was the early 1980s, and I had whiffed several house payments up my nose.

In 1984, I moved into a really nice apartment in Santa Ana. I didn't know anyone there, and no one from my past came by either. My associations cleaned up, although I still listen to Heavy Metal even to this day. I was breaking all ties to my old associations.

Then, on Labor Day 1984, I met my future wife of 30 years in the Jacuzzi. Sorry, that's another story that won't be told here. Martha Ann was my tipping point. I was told specifically by Martha Ann, "I don't do drugs, and I do not smoke."

Thank God she put her foot down and held her boundaries. It was either do drugs, or be with this woman. Martha Ann saved my life, and I didn't know it at the time.

We were so much alike, and she liked Heavy Metal, too.

When we went out to eat we would order the number 1 choice and the number 2 choice, and then share. Because if we didn't we would have ordered the same thing. She laughed at my jokes, and I laughed at hers.

I loved to make her laugh no matter how silly the joke. Life was great for both of us. I even started taking ceramics classes in 1999. Another new group of associations, and this time a better group, too.

In January 2003, just four days before I was leaving for Peru, I got laid off from my great paying job as a Senior Programmer Analyst. I went anyway, screw them. Martha was always the trooper, she told me to go ahead and have fun. I'd wanted to go to Peru and Machu Picchu since my early 20s, and Martha knew that.

During this time I had my first gallery showing in Santa Barbara, demos at the Orange County Fair, and won several awards in the Fine Arts competition at the Orange County Fair.

Life was good, and later I realized how quickly it can change without warning.

In 2006, a bunch of us potters went to the ocean side of Catalina Island to do a "pit firing" using buffalo chips as fuel. We were given a garbage bag and some garden gloves and told to go collect buffalo chips. I asked, which ones do we gather? My great teacher, Stella Vognar, said if you kick it and it moves, then get that one—yuck. This was pre-cell phone days, and there was a single payphone close to our campsite that took quarters.

I tried calling Martha several times that day, and she wouldn't answer the phone until later that night. Then, on the last day she kept asking, "where are you and when are you coming home?" I had been planning this trip to Catalina for months. I realized I had a problem to fix when I got home.

The day that I brought Martha to her doctor she must have asked 15 times, "Where are we going?" within the first hour. Since getting laid off from work, she had become very sedentary and was now walking very slowly. In the next days that followed there were tests, MRIs, draw a clock, who is the president of the United States? etc. The doctor came back and said, "Well, it's not Alzheimer's, but it is some kind of dementia." All I could think at the time was, "Thanks a lot."

What a turning and tipping point.

In order to keep my own sanity, I reconciled that I was a single parent now. And also, that some single parents have it a lot tougher than I did. I went from "Lover" to "Caregiver" in an instant. Martha loved music and sports, so I got all of those cable channels.

What's great about dementia is that you can watch a game and thoroughly enjoy it, watch the post-game show, and then watch the replay of the same game. You'll enjoy the replay "as if" it is brand new, because you don't remembering watching it in the first place. What a blessing.

Richard Barrier is an Entrepreneur, Speaker, Author, Ceramic Artist, Phone App Developer, and studies Pa-Kua. Richard speaks on Distracted Driving, what it is, why it happens, and why people are addicted to the Drug of Approval.

www.TXTMEL8R.com

THERE IS NOTHING LIKE A DREAM TO CREATE THE FUTURE—PART TWO

by Richard Barrier

S hortly after Martha's diagnosis, and two and a half years of unemployment, I got a job as a Computer Operator at the local community college. This was a job that I did when I first started working with computers in 1978. The school was close enough that I could go home at lunch and wake Martha up. I would then fix her lunch before going back to work. Martha loved to watch the old TV shows from the '50s, '60s, and '70s. The TV became her babysitter, and her cat, Princess, was always in her lap keeping her company.

I was warned that this job was going away in about three years. They were going through a system conversion to newer technology. I thought...great, I'll prove myself here, and then when the conversion is completed I will be transferred to the "systems" group. I would be back on top!

Then the Great Recession hit and the whole department was shut down in October 2009. I knew that I would have to re-invent myself at the age of 52.

I took night classes so I could take care of Martha during the day. After three years I had received three business degrees and had started a business that failed. My mother passed away, and I was the executor of her estate, dealt with crazy family issues, sold my mom's house, and started my current company.

The company is called Over the Top Projects LLC. I started to create a phone app called TXT ME L8R that saves lives by preventing adults and teenagers from using their phone while they drive. It's a solution for distracted driving, www.TXTMEL8R.com.

In 2013, I bought season tickets to ten Angels games. Martha Ann loved all sports. At the very first game, I caught Martha slowly swaying her shoulders during a Led Zeppelin song and enjoying a beer—thank you God. As the season progressed, I could tell that Martha's health was deteriorating. She was getting less responsive and having issues with the bathroom.

In early 2014, after I was able to get Martha Ann to take a bath. I noticed a deformity in her left breast. I had another problem to solve…it was breast cancer. I was told because of her age and health that she would not survive chemo. She could do hormonal treatment. The tumor shrunk by 40 percent, until it came back with a vengeance.

Martha Ann had a body scan, and one week later was her next doctor's appointment. Her doctor called me three days later—the cancer had metastasized.

When he saw her three days later, Martha had mentally checked out. The doctor immediately spoke about hospice care. Then five days later, my wife, Martha Ann, passed away at home and in her own bed. I am truly blessed that I was next to Martha when she took her last breath, on Oct. 3, 2014.

So, now what? Martha was my wife and my WHY, I had to re-invent myself again, and I had no excuses at all, it was all on me.

I am so fortunate, blessed, and grateful to have my close friends. I have a really great assembly of associations.

I started to write this chapter on the one-year anniversary of Martha Ann's passing. There are fewer tears and shorter sighs these days. Some of these pages have those tears and sighs. All of the storms of my life have been resolved, now I just need to build a business and my life.

After four years in development, my phone app, TXT ME L8R, is done. Yeah, right. I'm working on an update right now.

On December 23, 2014, I ordered a brand new, fully loaded 2015 Mustang GT as a Christmas gift to myself. I was told it wouldn't be ready until March 11, 2015. I went to an event in San Diego where there was some fund raising. As soon as I put my hand on the check that I was going to write for a donation, my phone began to vibrate. I thought I had turned it off. It was March 4 when I got a call from the dealership; my car was ready for pickup. I was in San Diego, so I couldn't pick it up until the next day, on March 5, which was my birthday.

Like I said previously, I've been making pottery or ceramic art since 1999. So, in my new Mustang, I've driven to North Lake Tahoe for a workshop that I'd wanted to take for ten years. I've also driven to Flagstaff, Arizona, for a two-week class at Northern Arizona University on wood-fired ceramics and have driven to Sedona and the Grand Canyon.

Recently I was a vendor at the AAA Teen Driver Safety event; I gave away license plate frames that said "I'm Driving" "TXT ME L8R."

I've been interviewed by CBS in Texas for a weekly health segment about distracted driving and my app, TXT ME L8R. I was also a speaker at the Third Annual Distracted Driving Summit in Virginia. Next week I'm starting a marketing campaign with all the news stations in Orange County and Los Angeles County. I am also writing a collaborative book on distracted driving.

I know 2016 will be amazing; I'm doing my second marathon since 2010, my first cruise to the Caribbean, going to The Grand Turks, Curacao, and then to Aruba for the 10th Annual Marketers' Cruise. I'm climbing Mt. Kilimanjaro, the highest peak in Africa, on a six-day safari. Who wants to go to Africa?

It's been a long ride from free-basing cocaine, to 30 years of marriage, to building a phone app that saves lives by preventing adults and teenagers from using their phone while they drive, to climbing Mt. Kilimanjaro. My regrets are none, these life events made me who I am now. Embrace life, and be involved. Thank you again, Martha Ann, for saving my life.

Richard Barrier is an Entrepreneur, Speaker, Author, Ceramic Artist, Phone App Developer, and studies Pa-Kua. Richard speaks on Distracted Driving, what it is, why it happens, and why people are addicted to the Drug of Approval.

www.TXTMEL8R.com

40-YEAR JOURNEY TO SUCCESS—
PERSISTENCE WINS THE DAY

by Craig Batley

M y mother and father raised my three sisters and me during the 1950s and early 1960s. It was a simpler time, a carefree environment, instilling discipline, hard work, and a job well done in the home of my childhood.

My parents were children of the Great Depression, where one learned to pay cash for everything, if you borrowed tools you returned them in better condition than when you received them, and you respected your elders.

You also took pride in being self-sufficient, independent, and thrifty. My father taught me early in childhood the principle of being rewarded for a job well done. My parents planted the seeds for my future success. I put those principles to work by mowing yards in the summer, having a paper route, and collecting the monthly subscription fees from my customers. My first real job was working at a service station for $1.50/hour. I had many other jobs during my college years.

While in college, I began to see the possibility of business success for myself. After graduating with a BA in Business Administration, two years later I obtained an MBA emphasizing entrepreneurship, and I was ready to interview for a job with an eye toward future success. After five interviews and personality profile testing, I knew the corporate world was not for me.

51

I didn't want my future salary to be dictated or limited by corporate bureaucracy. I desired pay commensurate to my income producing performance. In the early 1970s, Bob Bebee was the most productive and highest paid salesman for SCM Corporation. He quit his job to become an entrepreneur, earning three times what he had been earning as the top salesman in a 1,000+ sales force. I modeled Bob Bebee.

Another early mentor, Frank Satter, told me, "You get what you ask for in life." I didn't fully understand what he meant until years later, but I decided to follow my heart (listening to that "still small voice") and struck out on my own. I didn't know what I was going to do, but I knew whatever it was I would be living in Southern California. Sometimes we don't know our ultimate destination, but our journey begins with that first step of faith. I had that yearning desire (not quite burning yet, but beginning to smolder) to break free from the yoke of predictability and family expectations. I decided to pursue possibility thinking instead of probability thinking. I made the decision to pack up and move from the Pacific Northwest in 1972 to Southern California—the land of opportunity—and ended up in Newport Beach.

There I met my next mentor and employer, a successful independent millionaire entrepreneur named Rudy Mariman. Rudy taught me the art of making cold calls—an invaluable business sales skill. After two years of apprenticeship with Rudy, I ventured out on my own as a novice real estate flipper.

I started buying and selling houses and small income properties. After hundreds of phone calls and a little elbow grease, my first "fixer" property turned a $42,000 profit.

I was on my way to becoming a millionaire through real estate investing, the proud owner of a dozen properties. However, I stopped listening to that "still small voice" and took a 13-year detour going into debt and opened real estate brokerage offices beginning in 1978. After years of owning real estate offices, closing thousands of real estate transactions, I unloaded my thriving, but marginally profitable, multimillion dollar company in 1991. After paying off debt, there wasn't much left. I was no longer a millionaire and had to start over.

Prior to making decisions, it helps if you listen to that "still small voice," or that "whisper"—if you listen, good results will always occur. I made the decision to stay in the real estate business, entering the arena of property management, a cash flow business.

With a partner, we bought a small company in 1997 on the Balboa Peninsula in Newport Beach, a company that had been in business continuously in the same location since 1967. Almost 18 years later, the business has grown by 800 percent, and we own the property on which the business began 48 years ago.

What are the lessons to be learned from my 40 years in the business? The five basic lessons I have learned to become a successful entrepreneur are:

Lesson one. Never ever go into personal debt. In other words, it is not wise to borrow your way to success. Does that mean one cannot sell equity shares in your company? No. Does that mean one should not seek venture capital? No. There are exceptions, but ideally, I recommend not being personally liable for business debt. Instead, grow organically. Grow your company to success.

Lesson two. Especially, in the beginning, learn to ask for the order. Sell your product 24/7. If you cannot sell your product, then who can? Become your company's best advocate for your product or service.

Lesson three. Be persistent. Persistence wins the prize every time. Never give up. Believe you have the best product or service. Make dozens of calls a day. Sell, then sell some more.

Lesson four. Hire good people. Hire employees who are team players. Hire people who believe in you. Hire people who complement your skills. Hire people who are enthusiastic and want the company to be successful.

Lesson five. We live in a technological world. We must innovate and stay ahead of the competition.

How did I become a 43-year "overnight" success? I became a success by dogged determination and overcoming all the obstacles and setbacks that seemingly block the road to all those who seek success. Success is something you grow into after learning from your mistakes. Along the way I made hundreds of mistakes. Remember, success can be just around the corner, it can be the next phone call or next appointment. Do not give up. Do not procrastinate. Make that phone call today. Persistent action will bring success to you, too.

Established in 1967, Craig Batley owns Burr White Realty, a boutique full service real estate office specializing in vacation rentals, property management, and sales in Newport Beach and Orange County California.

www.Burrwhite.com

Awakening to My Destiny

by Stephen C. Carpenter

R emember the intro scene in "Enter the Dragon" where Bruce Lee is teaching his student Lau and says, "Kick me," to the student who nervously complies? Master Bruce coaches his student, who then enters the flow and executes the kicks properly. Bruce asks his student, "How did it feel?" The student replies, "Hmm, let me think," while reaching to his chin. Bruce whacks him one good and asserts, "Don't think! Feel! It is like a finger pointing a way to the moon." Lau proceeds to stare at the pointing finger of Master Bruce who teaches, "Don't concentrate on the finger or you will miss all of the heavenly glory!"

I spent the first 47 years of my life accumulating information and staring at the finger. On November 8, 2013, I was awakened in an instant by the most powerful storm ever to make landfall in recorded human history. Typhoon Yolanda descended upon the Philippines with a fury that day, and my pregnant wife and baby girl were residing there in Tacloban City, right in the eye of the storm. Where was I? I was across the Pacific at a RockStar MasterMind event and working full time as an EHS professional to support my family.

The people who truly matter the most to me in life were in the most dangerous situation imaginable. We had put together the perfect plan, but the universe thought differently. Finally after 72 hours, I learned my family had survived the storm! I thank GOD Almighty for protecting and guiding my loved ones safely through the storm. Within days I flew to Cebu City and was reunited with my beautiful family. When I hugged my family at the Mactan Airport, our tears flowed in a river of gratitude and love for survival in the midst of such profound devastation.

We lost many friends and some extended family members in Typhoon Yolanda. The place where the children used to play became like a tree where the lovely songbirds had flown away. As brave countrymen led relief missions into the disaster zone, they saw the devastation, the suffering, the survival, and the resilience of the people. The stories that came out of the disaster zone are a testament to the powerful and heroic nature of human beings. The stories and encounters changed me.

Many brave human beings gave their lives so that others could survive. It is phenomenal that human beings are willing to risk it all to save people they often do not even know! I believe this is a testament to our true nature. Human beings are powerful, blessed, sacred, spiritual beings connected intimately to source energy. I AM convinced more than ever of our divine nature. I know that human beings are wondrously made.

When Typhoon Yolanda slammed into the Philippines, I was awakened from my wave spell of conditioned mind complacency victim consciousness doldrums. The storm literally refreshed my memory that my mission here on earth is to serve humanity in positive and beneficial ways. This means practicing present moment awareness, for example, and being disciplined about fulfilling my dreams.

I see now that my work as an EHS professional in the trenches of corporate America through the years has always been aligned with my life mission. Where I had previously felt corporate conflict, I now appreciate a deeper sense of my role and its importance in the workplace. After all, I work to ensure that all employees go home safe and healthy to their families after their work shifts. That sincerely matters. When workers get hurt on the job, their families and loved ones suffer the true burden of the costs. Considering how all incidents in the workplace are preventable, this is where the tire truly hits the road. It is ALL about the family.

Today I work as an owner's representative EHS Manager on the biggest construction project in the United States of America. Our team works tirelessly to ensure the safety and health of more than 3,000 workers building the mother ship for surely one of the most successful companies on the planet. I AM honored to be part of the visionary, dynamic project execution team.

I recently published a concise safety leadership book entitled "Your Amazing Itty Bitty Safety Book: 15 Essential Steps for the Safe & Healthy Workplace Environment." The book encapsulates my vision for proactive risk mitigation and articulates an approach to building and sustaining a strong safety culture in organizations. I love talking about safety and health, and the book fortunately catalyzes motivational speaking opportunities for me. I AM quite thankful, as this is where my heart truly sings.

To be honest with you, I also have the dream to reforest planet earth. This focuses on the solution. Naturally, I plan to start the global reforestation mission in the Philippines, precisely where Typhoon Yolanda made landfall. At present I AM proposing to crowd fund the endeavor, known as the Global Reforestation Foundation Kawayan Bamboo Initiative. The reforestation endeavor centers on engaging local communities in planting 1 billion or more propagules, seedlings, and saplings of endemic bamboo, mangrove, and hardwood species.

The reforestation mission aims to provide a greater degree of protection to communities against future natural disasters while creating quality livelihood opportunities. This is especially important for youths and future generations. The reforestation work honors both the survivors and those people who lost their lives in Typhoon Yolanda. It represents a healing opportunity and a vital mission to support the countless families and children who are still suffering today there in the eye of the storm.

I AM forever grateful to be united with my wife, daughter and son. I honor the epiphany of love. I remember our first embrace together after Typhoon Yolanda and gazing up into the night sky to see the moon waxing in all of the heavenly glory. The teacher says to expect miracles, and miracles will happen. Thank GOD for teachers. Thank GOD for miracles. I AM Grateful.

Stephen C. Carpenter, MPH, CSP is an occupational and environmental health & safety (EHS) professional, author, motivational speaker, and coach. He works with people around the world to create safe and healthy workplace environments and generate those powerful win-win-win outcomes for stakeholders. Safety is truly a family matter. Stay safe and healthy!

www.AmazingSafety.com

ROCK BOTTOM TO ROCKSTAR

by Sandra Champlain

I was so nervous as my plane landed in Phoenix! It was my first occasion to be the "keynote speaker" at a large conference. Months prior, a woman had told me that my book "changed her life," and she asked me to share my story on stage.

A suite was reserved in my honor at a fancy hotel in Scottsdale, Arizona. I got VIP treatment but inside I felt like a fraud, so scared that my words would not be good enough for her audience.

She introduced me on stage, and suddenly 400 people were staring at me. I could see sadness in many eyes. I knew they were looking to me for answers.

My heart was racing, and my knees were shaking. I was honest and with a trembling voice said, "Good morning. I'm Sandra Champlain, author of the book 'We Don't Die,' and I am very nervous right now!" They laughed.

I took a deep breath, and for the next hour I shared my very personal story of fear and heartache. I told them about the fear of dying taking over in my life, for no apparent reason, back in 1996, and how I began searching for answers. I studied major world religions as well as "taboo" subjects like reincarnation, near-death experiences, and psychic phenomena. I studied doctors, scientists, and mediums who had astonishing stories of life after death.

I mustered up every bit of courage to tell them of the two personal, mind-blowing experiences I had had, that finally convinced me that life after death was real and that ended my fear. I saw their jaws drop, and I was certain someone would laugh or walk out of the room. But they did not. The room was so quiet you could hear a pin drop. Although I had had these incredible experiences that could help comfort many people, I was too afraid at of laughed at, or losing friends or family, so I never told anyone. Feeling ashamed, I told the audience that I kept this secret for over ten years.

January 2010 brought a blow to my family when my dad was diagnosed with cancer. May 11th of that year was the day Dad took his last breath. The months before his death were extremely painful. Not only did I witness the father I loved deteriorating and suffering from unimaginable pain, but major arguments began with my siblings. I became the "black sheep" of the family that I once believed would support each other through all the tough times.

Along with Dad dying on that day, deaths occurred in the relationships I had with my brother and sisters. They wrote me off, and I was also no longer able to see my nieces and nephew.

Depression seemed to take over, and I felt that I had hit rock bottom. I was not about to commit suicide, but I was in such a dark place that I could understand why others would end their lives in this kind of pain. There was no joy in my life, only sorrow and a pain that was deep in my belly. The tears never seemed to end.

I told the audience that the following question came into my mind: "Are these problems and pain and suffering all due to 'grief'?"

I began to read every bit of information I could find about what happens in the brain and get answers on why we must grieve. After months of digging, I found exactly what I was looking for! Our brain chemistry does change when we lose a loved one, and our system goes haywire for a long while. All those sleepless nights, the tears, the anger, even memory and perception changes happen during the grieving process. This explained the arguments; we were fighting about things that had not actually occurred as we believed they did! I also found some valuable tools to help ease my pain.

I recorded a free one-hour audio and called it, "How to Survive Grief" and posted it on survivegrief.com. Within months, the audio had been heard by several thousand people worldwide. I received emails that not only had my words helped alleviate pain, but people reported choosing not to commit suicide. I now had the moral responsibility that I needed to share these powerful words with a much larger audience. I wanted to write a book!

A conference I attended introduced me to Craig Duswalt. I learned that my words do matter and began my courageous journey as an author. I titled my book "We Don't Die—A Skeptic's Discovery of Life After Death." It was time to tell the world my story. Chapter 10 of the book contains the same words that are in my grief audio. I would teach people about grief, because people needed to learn. "We Don't Die" has become a #1 international bestseller, and a reader filmed a documentary about me! Life-changing and life-saving emails continue to arrive in my mailbox.

I closed my speech in Scottsdale after sharing my truest belief: "Life is an education for the soul for you to love, learn, forgive and have many emotional experiences. Please make your life count, go after your dreams, and play full out! Get your money's worth out of life."

I felt like a rock star in that moment. Four hundred people gave me a standing ovation and cheered. When it was over, a huge line formed of people wanting their picture taken with me or wanting my autograph.

Inside my head I still have doubts and fears and often forget about that day, even though I have felt like a rock star many times since that happened! Luckily, I know I shall never develop a big ego; I stay grounded and let my passion for making a difference with others fuel my actions. The toughest of times are often what it takes for us to find our passion and ignite our inner rock star.

Sandra Champlain is a highly respected entrepreneur, radio host, and author of the #1 international bestselling book, We Don't Die—A Skeptic's Discovery of Life After Death. Sandra is committed to making a difference in the lives of others and believes that every dream is possible.

www.sandrachamplain.com

THE BEDROCK BOOKKEEPING SUCCESS STORY—THERE ARE NO COINCIDENCES

by Joe DiChiara

When I was 17, I was tricked by my Dad into becoming a CPA. He told me that CPAs run businesses, and that's what I wanted to do. I never thought about anything else except becoming a CPA. Talk about focus; I never realized I had another choice. Little did I know that decision would bring me to a place called Oswego, New York. Oswego had its own climate, three feet of snow and 15 below.

During one summer break my grandfather told me to call this guy, Vince. All Gramps knew was that he was a CPA, and he was going to help me. I had no idea why, and I really didn't feel like trekking into NYC. I went begrudgingly. Vince turned out to be a great guy! He told me something that would impact my entire life. It was a simple statement. Vince said, "Why don't you join a fraternity?" It turned out that a lot of the conversations I had with Vince resonated with me.

In January of 1982 I met Mike B., and he belonged to a fraternity called Sigma Gamma. I decided I was joining and Mike started introducing me to some of his fraternity brothers. It was just like when I decided to become a CPA, I never thought twice about it. That was until I overheard heard one of my future brothers say, "I don't think the bros are going to have the pledges eat live worms this time." That was the first thing I ever heard Craig Duswalt say.

My years up in Oswego were a great time in my life, and being a part of Sigma Gamma was a big part of it. Craig and I enjoyed a special time in college. There wasn't anywhere in the world that threw better parties than Sigma Gamma. Was I glad I had listened to Vinny D.

Craig and I graduated from Otech and went our separate ways. I remember when he got his job with the band Air Supply, and I asked him how the heck he got a gig like that. He actually shrugged his shoulders and said "I don't know." He knows now and it's one of his mantras: "Show up" and "You never know who's watching." That was the last time I would see Craig for almost 25 years.

I became a CPA, got married, bought a house, and had three kids. I never really got to run any businesses like my father said I would. To my chagrin, I looked at what I had been doing, and I realized that I was an accountant, and I resented my Dad for tricking me into this. I wasn't happy. That wasn't what I had in mind, and I spent years trying all kinds of crazy entrepreneurial endeavors. There was the scanning business, the car stereo business, the ceramic jewelry business, Melaleuca, Talk of the Planet, and I even sold one of my CPA practices to become a database programmer. I always wound up back in public accounting.

In July of 2003 I came up with an idea that stuck. Remote bookkeeping. It worked, it was profitable, and it was different than being a CPA, which I really didn't want to be. In 2008 I teamed up with a client, and we tried to expand the bookkeeping business. I needed to teach people my system, so I wrote a course and started teaching it. The course worked but the business didn't. I was back to square one. If I had to be an accountant, it was going to be part time, so I started a coaching business.

Enter Mr. Duswalt. Craig had finished his tour with Air Supply and the last I had heard was he was touring with Guns and Roses.

Craig had started the RockStar Marketing Success System, and I was a little concerned. Obviously, his career was on the downside. He kept inviting me to his RockStar Marketing BootCamp. "Gamma bros get in for free," he said. After about a year of trying to duck him, I relented. He was a Brother and obviously needed my help. Why else would he keep asking me to come for free?

I've been to seven RockStar Marketing BootCamps now, and I spent over $10,000 at that first one. Free was a good marketing method. Craig did need my help but not the way I thought he needed it. That was September of 2012, and today I have a totally different mindset. I no longer resent my dad for tricking me into becoming a CPA. In fact, I am on the path to the kind of success I dreamed of when I was 17.

I'm grateful for all the seemingly useless pain and suffering I endured gaining the invaluable experience I have today. I am not only running several businesses—I help other entrepreneurs run their businesses. My greatest endeavor to date, Bedrock Bookkeepers Online Academy, is the result of being a member of Craig Duswalt's RockStar MasterMind. It would have never happened had I not taken that seemingly casual suggestion by Vinny D. "Why don't you join a fraternity?" Looking back on all of these little links and insignificant little seeds planted in my stubborn entrepreneurial brain, I have to ask myself, were these just coincidences?

I don't believe in coincidences anymore. I believe that God reveals himself through people and those little things they say that seem to get lodged into your subconscious and drive you for no logical reason. Becoming a CPA, meeting Vinny D., going to Oswego, joining a fraternity, reconnecting with Craig and traveling to Los Angeles because I thought I could help him. There was almost no logical thinking involved in any of these decisions. I did all of them because I just felt like I was supposed to. Success is a funny thing. Sometimes it happens just because it's supposed to. There are no coincidences!

––––––––––

Joe DiChiara is a CPA and serial entrepreneur. He has worked with thousands of small business owners over his 30+ years in public accounting—from startups, to bookkeeping and complex tax problems. Joe is an author, speaker, and business coach to accountants, bookkeepers, and like-minded entrepreneurs.

www.bedrockbookkeepersonlineacademy.com

How I Took Back My Life

by Roger Anthony Dumadag

At the age of 32, a former accountant and having spent four years of studying acting and performing theater in New York, I decided to pursue my dreams of being a professional actor in Los Angeles. Just like many other actors in L.A., the road was more than difficult. To begin with, I dragged with me credit card debt of over $30,000. Before leaving New Jersey, I'll never forget packing pennies into those brown cover rolls, with each roll amounting to only fifty cents each. My parents were certainly worried about me. I was always the dreamer and rebel.

However, my stay in L.A. that first year was far from how I had imagined it would be. Not that I would be suddenly successful, but my financial situation was almost destitute. I worked at different restaurants as a host, busser, and server. I remember one lunch shift at the Hamburger Hamlet in Sherman Oaks, where I had two tables and walked away with ten dollars after that shift.

My living situation was not any better. I had moved around five times with different roommates, from sleeping on a sofa to sleeping on floors, using my comforter as a sleeping bag. I became worried when my Ford Escort broke down. It was much cheaper to junk my car than get it fixed. For a while, I had to take a bus from South Pasadena to downtown L.A. and switch to another bus to go to Sherman Oaks, which took two hours each way. It might've been cheaper to stay home.

My credit card debt kept growing because I couldn't afford to make payments, so I rotated credit cards, paying one with another one and so forth. Didn't anyone else do that? The other problem was I was incurring high finance charges. It was sheer lunacy, but I was hard headed and couldn't see the forest for the trees. I began to feel hopeless and depressed, because I couldn't even concentrate on my acting career, which was non-existent, even though casting directors told me I was talented. One thing that saved me in L.A. was my faith in God.

So I decided to go back home East with no car, no job, no career, and no relationship. I would have been living on Skid Row in downtown L.A. if I didn't get my act together. Thank God my parents were there for me. I moved back into my old basement bedroom. At 33, I thought my life would be different…with a career that I loved, a relationship, my own home, money in the bank. Instead, I had nothing except was now $40,000 in debt.

When I returned home I didn't have a game plan, and my mindset wasn't strong. My brother Pat suggested listening to Tony Robbins. Now I knew Tony Robbins was a big infomercial guru back in the 80s selling his cassette program "Personal Power." So I decided, hey you know what, what do I have to lose? I started listening to his cassette tapes over and over again. I figured I'd just brainwash myself positively. I felt that my attitude started to change. I started to make goals for myself. I started to watch TPN, The People's Network, a channel on a TV satellite service that offered personal growth development programming.

I watched people like Brian Tracy, Barbara DeAngelis, Les Brown, and many other personal growth gurus, coaches, and mentors who were powerful and inspiring. I felt more positive about my outlook on life, and I believed I could achieve anything if I set my mind to it. This was the beginning of my journey to not only take back my life, but to inspire others, and with the law of attraction many positive things started to happen.

One of my goals that I really wanted to achieve was to pay off my huge credit card debt of $40,000. I worked at a catering staffing company in New York. The owner noticed how hard I was working as a captain, and when the opportunity arose, I asked for more responsibilities and got a promotion and huge raise.

For the first time in my life I was making a six-figure income three years from almost being homeless. Within two years, I had paid off all my credit card debt. I began to improve my credit rating and even started saving and investing in stocks. I was able to qualify for my first mortgage and own my first real estate property. I bought my first car in years!

Five years later, I continued my personal development journey with the company Peak Potentials after my brother Pat introduced me to the book "Secrets of the Millionaire Mind." The next ten years I took more courses and attended camps, became more enlightened, networked my butt off, and many more wonderful and beautiful things happened. My mindset began to transform exponentially.

Along the way, I opened my own staffing company in New York and sold it seven years later. I owned and managed a few real estate properties. I began another business of helping people with their overall health. My investment portfolio and net worth began to grow to where I'm financially free now. But the most important event on this journey happened when I met a beautiful woman at the Seminar of the Century in Aspen—a sort of Woodstock for the best minds in the world. We dated after that, I asked her to marry me the following year, and our marriage has been blessed with love and abundance in every way. I had invoked the law of attraction. Literally.

I'm blessed and grateful for all the wealth, health, and beautiful relationships that continue to grow. And now because I'm financially free, the best part is I get to help people and inspire others to live their healthiest through my Kangen Water® business. And even better, on my creative side, I get to write, direct, produce, and act in film and TV projects that I had always wanted to do.

My book "Take Back Your Life Now" is due out soon, and I hope to inspire millions to do exactly that.

———————

Roger Anthony Dumadag is a global health and wellness advocate and coach as well as a professional actor, filmmaker, producer, singer, and musician. Roger's mission is to help people improve their overall health and wellness through Kangen Water® and living a more healthy and happy lifestyle.

www.Aquamazing.com

A ROCKSTAR STRATEGY
THROUGH THE VOICE OF GOD?

by Maryann Ehmann

I was so tired of it. Literally. My mind and body ached from sleepless nights worrying about our dwindling finances. Losing our home and living in a cardboard box under a bridge was looking more and more like our future reality. I'm not exaggerating.

Just a few years prior, we had taken the leap and moved into our country estate with lush and bountiful gardens, manicured lawns, and wildlife to greet us each morning. This property was beyond my dreams. Meeting the higher mortgage and expenses was no problem, as our business more than supported the increase.

Life was good.

And then, to our horror, 9/11 occurred. As with many others, fear invaded our hearts, while we watched the devastation. It became clear that the attack on the world's financial center was strategically designed to cripple the finances of the US, but never did we expect to personally feel the ripple in our business. One by one, my husband lost his insurance company clients as they decided to discontinue using outside investigators to cut costs.

At first we thought this shift was just another little dip in the road from which we would recover in a short period, just as we had so many other times. Business has its ups and downs, and typically, if you stay positive, plan, and adjust, the road smooths out eventually.

But one month turned into six, which turned into twelve, and after three years of income one-third of what it had been, we could no longer stave off the creditors or rob Peter to pay Paul. Peter was broke.

One thing about ongoing crisis is it can bring you to your knees in desperate prayer, and believe me we were doing that as we sought a strategy to change things.

But nothing was changing.

Our old methods of seeking God's help were no longer working. "What the heck?" I felt abandoned, alone, and victimized by an economy we couldn't control.

"What are we missing? It's not supposed to be this way? We both have doctorates, for crying out loud!" More self-pity and resentment clouded my mind.

And then a moment of clarity came: I saw that my faith was not in an upward swing but in our inevitable decline.

"As your faith is, so shall it be."

Faith has a direction, and I did not like where ours was headed.

So we studied the will of God about finances, prosperity, and business success and learned that our mindsets were messed up! It wasn't the economy that was the problem; it was our beliefs! This revelation empowered me. Faith rose up that relief would come. I didn't know how or when, but for the first time in years, I was certain a solution would appear.

One day while listening to one of our favorite teachers share how his wife secured just the right job after writing down her requirements, something spoke to my soul. Could it be that we could actually write down our desires and…get them? That seemed wrong. I had been warned about treating God like a Santa Claus. Was that what this teacher was promoting?

Not at all. I realized in that instant, that God had already given us all the provisions for an abundant life, and our job was to access it. Not beg, borrow, or steal. But simply access it.

Just at that moment, a gentle whisper instructed my heart, saying, "Write down how much you and Gene want and don't skimp. I am a God of more than enough, and it is all yours."

Filled with excitement and apprehension, I ran to Gene and told him what I had heard. "You write down an amount, and I will, too, and let's see if they are the same!" And so we did.

Thinking about all the things that had fallen into disrepair, the mounting debt, not being able to visit our daughter and family in England, "go big or go home" raced through my mind like I was writing our ticket to Adventure Land. I didn't second guess it, refusing to even think what my husband might write.

OMG! It was exactly the same as mine.

A few days later my husband received a contract for work that would cover fifty percent of the dollar amount to which we were committed. Though it increased our current revenues, and it was an "out of the blue" offer, it wasn't enough to match the amount we had written. He declined.

"Was this craziness? Turning down an offer that was almost twice as much as our current income?"

No, it was wisdom. To follow the voice of God and His leading seems nuts in our day and age. But is it?

We are smart people. But our smarts did not keep us from getting into a deep financial hole or help find a way to get us out.

No. We needed something bigger than ourselves.

We needed an out of the box, rock star strategy.

Who knew it would be through the voice of God?!

Confidence and peace replaced my anxiety-riddled nights, even before the money was in the bank! My husband put a stake in the ground when he said no. And guess what? They came back with another 25 percent increase. The remaining 25 percent came easy with my help.

After years of inadequate revenues, more than 100 percent of our number came into our bank accounts each and every month. Following that, we received even more.

We paid off debt, repaired and improved the house, took a wonderful family trip to Europe (two, in fact), purchased sorely needed new cars, and abounded in excess of our expenses.

Unbeknownst to us, God was giving us the keys to manifesting our dreams and desires: Honor them, listen to Him, set your intention, and take action. As our renewed mindset has continued to upgrade, and so has our life. Change your beliefs, change your results!

———

Maryann Ehmann is a professional speaker, radio show host, success coach, and creator of Create Your Magnificent Life Now. Maryann inspires and coaches entrepreneurs, professionals, and ministry leaders to live a life beyond their dreams by strengthening the beliefs they need to achieve the results they desire.

www.maryannehmann.com

HOW I OVERCAME FEAR TO ACHIEVE SUCCESS AND HAPPINESS

by Linda Fleischmann

I had worked in banking for over 13 years, and after the multiple mergers in the industry, I decided to move to a new profession. I had had some experience with mortgage loans, so I ended up at a mortgage company that did subprime loans. After three months with them, I was laid off and decided to become self-employed.

I started my own company and had my former assistant manager as my partner. After six years of working with her, I found I was bringing in 90 percent of the revenue and she was getting half of the income. So I decided to end that partnership—but ended up with another partner.

What I was missing was that I was fearful of being alone and running a business by myself. At that time, we had ten loan officers, two processors, and an assistant. I was running both the business end of the company as well as bringing in 75 percent of the loans. But I was afraid of doing this alone, without a partner to discuss the different issues that arose. My husband, Mark, is a business consultant and CFO and has extensive knowledge in all areas of business. As he saw me struggling with the business, he saw what I couldn't. I was relying on people that were never going to be there for me, and I was paying for friendship.

As the financial markets were decimated in 2007, the mortgage industry fell apart. I was forced to downsize and move to a smaller location with just my partner and a few loan officers.

During that time, no matter the amount of loans that I closed, I was not getting paid. All of the income was put back into the company. In 2006, the company with over ten loan officers closed 53 million dollars total, and of that, I closed loans totaling 24 million dollars.

In 2008, my partner was working as our processor, and we didn't have any staff. I was able to close 17 million dollars myself, but by 2009, I took home in pay a total of $2,000 for the year.

In 2010, I was networking and got very involved in a women's group where we had monthly speakers. I had heard many speakers, all interesting, but there was only one that seemed to speak to me, and he was talking about writing a book in 30 days.

I had NEVER had any desire to write a book, but that seemed to make sense to me. Talk about what you know, and you become an expert in that field by writing a book. So I wrote a book called "How to Have a Stress Free Mortgage, Insider Tips from a Certified Mortgage Broker to Help Save You Time, Money and Frustration." That was a real accomplishment and made me feel like I was giving back.

These were very difficult years in the mortgage industry with many changes, and having to worry about compliance, administration and employees, along with closing the loans, was very stressful.

My partner had married and had a baby as well. Her hours became 9 to 5, and mine were 7 to 7 most days to try to keep up with the volume. My husband kept telling me that I should be on my own, but I was still held captive by the fear of being alone. The other part that kept me from doing anything was that this was MY company; I had built it from nothing. We had a great reputation in the city I was in, and I couldn't fathom not having the company I had built. This was about emotion, not logic, and it was hard to overcome the feelings.

But with the many changes the industry was facing, I started to think more and more about what it would be like to just do loans and not have to manage the company and the people.

We all have our place to where we get pushed and finally go over the edge, and in November of 2010, that point came. My partner had been invited to go to see "Ellen" with the other loan officer in the company. That morning, she came in early for once, at 7 a.m. instead of 9 since she was leaving at 11. I had a lot of loans I was working on, but since she was processing them, when she was gone, I had to do the processing as well. So, as I was in her office going over a few things, I was feeling the stress building and my anger as well.

I asked her if she had to go to see Ellen, and her reply was she didn't have to, but she wanted to…and in my head, I thought, "and I want to close loans." All my emotions came out and something inside snapped, and I was finally done. Done with her, done with the company, done with working for everyone—but me.

She came to me a few days later apologizing for the mistakes she had been making, and although I hadn't planned on it, I told her I was done. She looked at me confused and said, done? I said, yes, I'm closing the company and going on my own. And that was it. I finally got over my fear and did what I should have done years before.

In January of 2011, I took a few of the employees we had, closed Loan Connectors, and started my own company called Stress Free Mortgage.

It was the best decision I had ever made. In 2013, I closed 47 million dollars in loans, more loans than I had ever done in the past. The company my license is with takes care of all of the compliance and administration, and I have never been happier or more successful. Overcoming fear is difficult to do, but closing the company I built after 13 years was the right thing to do.

I have great people working for me, and I have my husband, Mark, who is the only partner I will ever have, both in business and life. That is my success and I am happy, financially strong, and doing what I was meant to do.

Linda Fleischmann started her company in the mortgage industry in 1999 and has helped thousands of clients both purchase homes and refinance their loans. Linda prides herself on her reputation as being able to get her loans closed with the least amount of stress for her clients.

www.stressfreemortgage.com

VISUAL REALITY

by Patricia Karen Gagic

T here was something very special about reading magazines when I was growing up in the mid-'60s. A form of enticement would reveal itself toward the last few advertisement pages. A company offered to critique your art work by way of drawing a silhouette of a woman's face and sending it to them. I am pretty sure I spent three years perfecting my image before mailing it. Sleepless nights followed as I anticipated receiving their response. I remember the feeling of being in complete awe as the carefully crafted letter revealed something to the effect "with training you have the potential to be an artist." I was 12 years old.

Years later, my desire to understand the laws and mechanics behind creating art never ceased. The passion took over. The world I existed in seemed unique, as my interests were strong and definite in more than one area. It was a balanced left side, right side world in which both the world of art and business co-existed. What became a profound sense of encouragement at the age of 12 also sealed a sense of confidence. Imagine, the impact of receiving words in a hand-written letter from someone who had the power to place an ad in a magazine! Well, life is not as predictable as we think, and yes, sometimes adjustments along the way interfere with our ability to do what we really want in life. Making a living as a female artist was not really an option, and I became a Banker.

Determined to keep the artistic fires burning, I joined art organizations, visited galleries, and ferociously read about the artists who inspired me. It was a joyful and promising fling through the art world, but something was missing. The scales were tipping as my soul yearned for more time in the gestation of creation. The business of business seemed to have conquered the ivory tower inside my head, and while I loved all aspects, my hands needed to work with different tools. The jump from pens to brushes was made easy. A birthday gift from my husband turned the tables of fate.

After years of being "present" in the art scene, I had established a few gallery representations and continued to exhibit regularly. Through a series of introductions, I had the fortune of meeting a lovely gallerist who invited me to consider joining the stable of artists he represented. On the day of our meeting, my husband preoccupied himself with securing an amazing rental home in France. My job was to meet the owner and tidy up the rental agreement.

Fortunately he lived close by, and I was invited to his home. There was a magical energy generating around this visit as everything seemed perfectly aligned. As we concluded, I noted that the art work in his home was outstanding. Notably one piece of work with a beautiful white horse immediately caught my eye, as it was non-traditional and somewhat etheric and abstract. The artist was Dragan Dragic. I fell in love with his work. The owner knew the artist, who lived in Savoillan, France, and was considered an icon in the Provencal area. The seed was planted—I must meet him. An attempt to contact Dragic would be made when we were in France.

While I was absolutely in love with every aspect of our location, the home and the landscape, my mind was focused on meeting the artist named Dragic. Several attempts were made to communicate with him, and finally he agreed to our rendezvous the following Thursday at two p.m. It was a three-hour drive south to Mt. Ventoux. We were given very precise directions. This journey included tricky exits on very winding roads.

If we missed the exits as shown on the map, we would be entering from the other side of the mountain, adding an additional hour and a half to our journey. We missed an exit, arriving two hours late. Fortunately, Monsieur Dragic waited patiently and welcomed us. Within a short period of time, we had established that my husband and Dragic grew up not far from one another's villages. This meeting was aligned by the stars!

For the first time in my life, I entered into the atelier of an artistic genius. The stone walls were covered with unfinished work, echoing a timelessness to their existence. The studio was built inside the turret of the fifth century home he had lived in for decades. There were no words to describe the magnificent art works on display.

My head was spinning, and I was grateful for this one moment in time created by the serendipity of circumstances. Dragic proudly shared many photos of himself with Picasso, Christo, and exhibitions throughout France and Switzerland. My passion to paint had been given a nuclear fuel boost. Leaving the atelier, my heart was racing with excitement along with a silent sadness knowing I would never be able to experience this moment again.

Walking us to our car, Dragic asked me why I painted. Is it for the money? Is it for the fame? Do you love creating more than anything else? He declared he was not a teacher yet was willing to invite me back. I returned six months later with canvas and paint in hand and established a deeply rewarding relationship with one of the world's greatest living artists.

The months and years have continued to flourish with time spent in his atelier, culminating in the greatest epic moment of my career, a joint exhibition in Sault, France, the pinnacle of success.

Our friendship has blossomed into a working hypothesis of respect and endurance. I am grateful and humbled by the genius of Dragan Dragic. His message was always clear: "Find the source of your wisdom, let it reveal itself, and always follow your heart."

———————

Patricia Gagic is an International Artist and award winning Author. She is a 2015 Top 100 WXN Most Powerful Women in Canada recipient and Dame of the Order of St. George. She is also a Certified Meditation Specialist in Applied Mindfulness and Transformative Mindfulness from the University of Toronto and the founder of The Karmic Revolution inspiring people to Master the Five Radical Degrees of Life.

www.InspiredtobeRewired.com

STAND UP AND SPEAK UP

by Walt Grassl

"If you're not going to speak up, how is the world supposed to know you exist?"

—Author unknown

In 2006, I had been working for a Fortune 500 company for over 30 years. I had advanced from test technician to Senior Engineering Manager. I led a department of 100 engineers. It looked like I was having a great career. But looks can be deceiving.

Annual performance reviews were consistently outstanding. Yet, there was a consistent opportunity for improvement—my communication skills.

Why? I suffered from leg shaking, hand shaking, perspiration dripping, dry mouth, mind going blank stage fright.

Stage fright appeared when presenting to peers, management, and customers. It also appeared in interviews for higher-level positions. Had I addressed stage fright earlier in my career, I would have risen higher and faster within the company.

In 2006, I had to deliver a critically important message to a group of our employees. My boss was in the audience and observed my less than stellar delivery. He called me into his office and told me I could no longer ignore the issue. He sent me to our HR manager to figure out a way to fix me, and he suggested I join the Toastmasters club at our facility.

77

I reluctantly joined Toastmasters, and my initial progress was slow. I only spoke six times in the first 18 months. Joining a group will not make you better. You have to do the work.

While I did not speak a lot, I attended Toastmasters speech contests to watch good speakers. In October 2007, I spoke to the keynote speaker at our District Conference before he gave his speech. I decided to invest in myself by purchasing his training materials.

In February of 2008, I made a bigger investment. I attended three speaker-training events in Las Vegas: Storytelling, Humor, and a general speaking seminar called Lady & the Champs.

During the humor seminar, I got up on stage to deliver a two-line joke I had just written a few minutes before. My mind went blank. I picked up my notes. My hands were shaking so bad, I had a hard time reading the joke. At the end of the event, I was frustrated to tears. It was suggested I try an open mic night. "If you get in front of a crowd and get even one laugh, you will learn to relax. Don't compare yourself to people who are at the top of their game. Look at others who are just starting out." Right!

At Lady & the Champs, I talked to attendees and presenters. I asked how they overcame stage fright. Nothing resonated with me. But I noticed that these speakers were NOT dripping with charisma. They were just like me, without the fear.

On the flight back home, I realized I had a long journey ahead of me, but I was determined to conquer stage fright. I set the goal of being good enough to get paid to speak by August of 2012, when I would be 55 and old enough to retire.

I vowed to speak at my Toastmasters club at least once a month. I joined three more clubs. I committed to speaking in all available Toastmaster speech contests. It was difficult at first, but the more I spoke, the easier it got. Repetition builds confidence.

At one of the contests, I heard about improv, which is unscripted comedy. I found a class and signed up. In improv, I struggled at first, trying to plan ahead and not being present in the moment. I learned to listen and trust that I could pull something out of my head to move the scene forward.

Next, I enrolled in a standup comedy class. I put together a five-minute comedy set to perform at the Hollywood Improv. Yikes!

On a Sunday night in March of 2009, I was at the Hollywood Improv. The show was open to the public. Two hundred people were well into their two-drink minimum. I thought, "What am I doing here?"

I was scared witless…literally. You see, halfway through my set, my mind blanked. I pulled my joke list out of my pocket, looked at it and put it back. Then I forgot what I had just read. I slowly pulled it out again, got a laugh and then finished my set.

I got laughs! I went from sheer terror to the most exhilarating moment of my life. What a rush.

After that, speaking in front of 200 sober Toastmasters was nothing. Ok, I was still scared—but much less so. Speaking at work was a piece of cake. Over time, I even performed in local improv and sketch comedy shows.

As August of 2012 approached, I felt I was good enough to get paid to speak. But, how? I joined a MasterMind group. I shared my story of overcoming stage fright and my MasterMind peers helped me develop Stand Up & Speak Up. They inspired me to host a radio show, write a book, and audition to get into the prestigious Groundlings School for improv and sketch comedy.

In February of 2015, I was at Lady & the Champs again. As I took my seat, the gentleman next to me said, "Are you Walt Grassl?"

He went on to say he was at the event because he heard about it on my radio show. He said he listened to the podcasts regularly. He found out about it in a Google search.

Wow. I was floored. Up until now, I thought only friends or friends of guests listened to the show. I felt like a "RockStar."

I began this incredible journey to face a fear and improve my career. Over time, I decided to encourage other people to overcome their fears. To learn that people are finding me and that I am making a difference just feels so good.

When will you stand up and speak up, and let the world know you exist?

Walt Grassl is a professional speaker, author, radio personality, and entertainer. Walt delivers his leadership message "Good Leaders Ask Dumb Questions" to corporate, collegiate, and conference audiences.

www.WaltGrassl.com

READY-FIRE-AIM!

by Sandra Hanesworth

You know what? The funny thing about success, in a book filled with people who are sharing their success stories, is that the very definition is all relative to the journey of the person who achieves it. The bottom line is that no matter what one person defines success as, in the end, only action can create success. With that in mind, I have built my business, A-List Connection, on the idea that we help professionals take action to reach the top, to be a success, in life, love, and finance.

There are plenty of my clients out there who will tell you that we are successful, especially because I have spent years putting every possible resource under one roof for anybody to come and use. We've built a team and the tools necessary to support our clients in defining and achieving success. To me, my actual success was in helping others figure out what tools they needed to be the success that they had defined—sometimes with my help, sometimes by themselves.

So in many ways, I am surrounded by successful people—which is awesome! We are able to get people the right connections, coaches, and planning and help them to lose the fear of making changes in their lives and to understand the best ways to impact their income and their mindset. I've found the secret to helping others is to provide the resources they need and support them in their action plan. Many times, this part can help to really alleviate the fear that people have as they begin a new life or engage one they haven't enjoyed in a long time.

Of course, the downside is that for some folks, the plan can get all-encompassing and then it replaces a real action to obtain real goals. That's why a huge part of our job is to help people to achieve whatever the goal is.

It really is the best job in the world, because even though people may come to us as a widow or widower, with a radically new financial picture and life, we can sit down and support them to think through, understand, and take action on a plan for the next one, three, and five years—which then supports them finding their bigger purpose. We get to be present when people lose the fear, finally break through and see the problems, then change their mindset and define what is going to make them a success according to their own beliefs.

Of course, the real irony is that despite being surrounded by success, and even being successful in many ways, I was so devoted to success in others that I forgot to put the focus on defining it in my own life. I was so busy helping others to get the right connections and sequences in their own journey that I was not on my own to-do list. There I was in the kitchen, and I didn't make time to eat my own cooking.

Enter Glenn Morshower. Three years ago, I heard Glenn speak at Craig Duswalt's event, and Glenn talked of listening to the "whispers" that come to you in your life and how they are really calls for action that you can choose to heed, or not. Glenn listened to those whispers, and the results were astounding in his life and success. I decided to take Glenn's advice and start paying attention to my own whispers, and in doing so, I redefined what success was to me. Was it fun? It was awesome!

The funny thing? The whispers I listened to told me it was time to take my company coast-to-coast, and that was just what I did. Plenty of folks thought I was acting randomly, in sort of a "Ready-Fire-Aim" mentality that trips up many people. But the whispers? They were telling me the things they knew that I hadn't thought of: My vision for A-List Connection has grown through the years, and I wanted to have a presence globally.

I had built a growth strategy, and because of my incredible joint-venture partners across the world, we had top-notch people to work with coast-to-coast, and in no time, we were perfectly aligned to dedicate my energy and passion to creating a national platform for how singles can thrive in their personal and business lives and have loads of fun while they build and define their own success.

I was so close to my own recipe for success that I couldn't see how well planned out it was; and indeed to many people, I made this huge move without a clear plan—rather randomly. In reality, I did this all by overcoming my fears and taking action. Simply put, I knew, at least in the back of my mind that all these pieces added up to success, but the real test was to jump in and do it. If I didn't get over the fear, or more likely, the second-guessing, I would never realize my newfound definition of success—play limitlessly!

That was why it was so empowering for me to basically decide—finally—to listen to the voices—the whispers—and take a second home in Fort Lauderdale and become "bi-coastal."

The whispers drove me to make all these connections, and as I learned to listen to them, I realized that I had known and felt the bigger purpose to connect with as many people as possible, and that I had already subconsciously built those connections that I needed for my business. More importantly, my mind had been refining my own definition of success so that when I finally took the time to listen to myself—really listen—I had built a system that was big enough and strong enough to live up to my dreams—I just had to take the time to realize that my success was going to be defined by how many people I can serve and that playing small was no longer an option. Taking concise action and having a great plan that includes partners and mentors is the key to A-List Success.

———————

Sandra Hanesworth is a professional speaker, author, and founder of A-List Connection LLC. Sandra creates conversations and experiences to elevate the health, wealth, travel, and love lives of single professionals globally. She is passionate about helping A-List single men and women live out their best 1-, 3-, and 5-year lifestyle plan…with no-regrets!

www.AListConnection.com

How an Accident Can Be a Blessing in Disguise

by Sheryl Hensel

WHAT IF…you had an understanding that all things in life, good and bad, are divinely provided for your opportunity to grow?

WHAT IF…you had an understanding that one slight tilt of the head can totally change your perception of any situation?

WHAT IF…you had an understanding that "control" of your life isn't what you think? How would that look and feel to you?

Can life be that simple that if we "go with the flow" everything will be okay? I am here as a testimony to say yes, it can be that simple…or not.

As a business-owner dedicated to transformative healing, my first priority is to establish a relationship of trust. I want my clients to feel confident that I will do my best to help them achieve their personal goals and that my life experiences have led me to be in the position to help.

My Story

I began a career as a middle school teacher, where I was drawn to the service of children and learning. I was on top of my game and recently promoted to the position of district-wide School-to-Work Coordinator. My path, however, took a totally new direction two years later in 1998.

Waiting at a stop light, I witnessed a car veer across traffic and crash onto the sidewalk. I rushed to assist the driver, and moments later while speaking with 911, I was struck by another motorist. I sustained a severe closed head injury and brain trauma. Despite extensive rehabilitation and Western medicine treatment, I continued to suffer from migraines, limited cognitive functioning, general pain, and depression.

The hardest part of it all was that I "looked" okay, but things weren't clicking inside. It's frustrating to know you just don't remember things like you used to, while visibly appearing to be fine. Years later, I grew to understand what a blessing that accident was to me.

Divine Intervention

The day after my accident a student brought a gun to the school where I taught and killed himself minutes before classes started. I was not meant to be there to witness the shooting, and have the screams my students told me of, scorched in my memory.

God knew that was one experience I didn't need to carry with me through life. I would have been one of the first on scene as his locker wasn't too far from my classroom. Shortly after the shooting occurred, I did go in and help counsel and console the kids. Such a traumatic experience demanded the comfort from those they trusted. On that day, I was very grateful for the accident that happened just the day before.

The Introduction to the "Cure"

A few years later, I left my medical support group and took a job in Florida as an Education Coordinator at a juvenile justice day treatment center. I took the risk of taking a new job thousands of miles from my family, by myself, and moved to a place where I didn't know a single person. God placed me in Florida for a reason. My first year into my new job, a student in our program lost his life to Russian roulette—another tragic loss I couldn't wrap my mind around at the time but was there for the kids. One of the greatest divine interventions that came from my move to Florida was the introduction of Quantum Energetics Structural Therapy (QEST). QEST fully relieved my symptoms, restored my cognitive abilities, and has become my life's passion.

Another Call to Serving Others

While living and teaching full time in Florida, I flew to Colorado every six weeks to learn the powerful healing work of QEST. Frankly, I couldn't afford to make these trips on a teacher's salary. However, I couldn't afford NOT to make them, and I didn't know why. A year after starting classes, one of the answers became obvious to me. My mother was diagnosed with stage 4 cancer...now it made sense. Ten years later, after many sessions, Mom is cancer free and takes ZERO medication.

Today I am a QEST practitioner! This scientific healing method corrects physical symptoms and emotional traumas at the root cause. This powerful work has helped restore physical, emotional, and spiritual health and create new vitality for clients with cancer, migraines, depression, and a myriad of other conditions (minor and major), where traditional approaches have failed. The QEST work all started with brain injuries and progressed from there.

A Little Fun along the Way

After the ending of my marriage, the divine guidance that came to me was to "go West," and my life brought me to California. Being part of the health and wellbeing industry, I added Cavi-Lipo to my business. This ultrasound, non-invasive solution to melt unwanted fat and cellulite resonated with my intention to help others avoid surgeries and drugs.

The Big Picture

I was angry because of the accident. WHAT IF I had not stopped to help someone. Had the accident not happened, I would not have been introduced to QEST and not able to help so many people.

I'm fortunate to have listened to that inner voice and not let fear paralyze me and keep me from growing. Life has shown me how little control I truly have. We all need not be victims when life is full of choices. On any given day, we can wake up and decide to have a good day or a bad day.

When I'm feeling bad about a situation, I think of three scenarios that shift my feelings into a positive state. Don't let your mind play games with you...just tilt your head, shift, and look at things differently.

My success is founded on strong integrative tools and intuitive talent, and I can't help but smile at the opportunity I get every day to share this. My love of God and belief that things are as they are meant to be has served me well. Have faith…trust the process…go with the flow. More than anything… follow your heart!

Sheryl Hensel is a professional speaker, author, CEO, and disease prevention practitioner. Sheryl works with people one-on-one, in groups, and with corporations. Her non-invasive approach assists people in shifting their health, looks, and perspectives. Sheryl is the owner of Sculpted Beauty, which is located in Costa Mesa, CA.

www.myfatmelted.com

Nothing Ventured, Nothing Gained

by Roxi Bahar Hewertson

A s a young, new manager at Cornell University, I was invited to attend a three-day orientation series. On the first day, Joan, a Vice Provost and the most senior woman at the university at the time, gave a talk that struck a deep chord within me. She said, "Never let anyone intimidate you, here or anywhere, in life. You have as much right to your opinion as anyone—as much ability to think good thoughts as anyone. No one has the right to intimidate you in any way." That concept deeply resonated with me and would soon be put to the test.

In later sessions, I heard several other senior people give three conflicting points of view about the university's core mission. At a break, I asked Jack, the powerful University Controller, which was the correct view. He literally wagged his finger just short of my nose and said, "Listen here, you don't know anything yet, so don't ask stupid questions!"

Well, I'm not all that keen on having fingers in my face to start with, and Joan's words were still echoing in my brain. So...I took what felt like a huge risk and put my hand up between his finger and my nose. I then calmly said, "Hang on, Jack; did you know that the people giving these sessions are sending three very different messages to us, and it's really confusing?" I gave him the facts, to which he replied, "Really? Oh, gee, I didn't realize that.

Thanks for telling me." And he wandered off. From then on, he treated me with respect, and I'm quite certain it was because I stood up for myself the first time he met me.

This was the beginning of what would turn out to be a life-long habit of taking risks. Risk-taking IS the main reason many of my visions for the future unfold. It is because I BELIEVE almost anything is possible. Letting go of fear, taking risks, and embracing life head-on can mean choosing between security and freedom. I choose freedom more often than security, and that means I take a fair number of risks.

I am aware that taking risks can be very scary. Even coming from a mindset of abundance and possibility, life events can wipe you out and knock you down, anxiety can cripple you, and worry can make you feel like you are going crazy. All of those things have happened to me more than once, and probably will again. And yet, our resilience can be grown and strengthened—indeed, every success, no matter how small, adds to our reservoir, and that can keep us going and going.

"Nothing ventured, nothing gained" is a liberating mantra. I say it often. I also ask myself, "What's the worst thing that could happen, and can I live with it?" Most of the time, the answer is, "Yes, I might not like it, but I will survive and rebound."

The first step in creating the future I want is being willing to take risks. I have to believe I am worth it, that I can do it, and that it is possible. I have to believe even when there is little or no logic to back me up. The next step is to ask myself the following four questions, no matter how big or small the vision:

Is it …

1. **Inspiring:** Is this vision worth committing my time and life force? Do I feel passionate about it? Does it give me the energy to do the day-in, day-out work? And might my vision inspire others when they hear me talk about it?
2. **Clear:** Do I have a clear picture of my desired results? Does it guide me as I create goals and evaluate my progress? When others hear my vision, do they get a clear picture of where I am going?
3. **Credible:** Does this vision stretch me and give me a sense of what's possible in the present? Will it pull me into a new and better future

even if it challenges some of my paradigms? Ultimately, is it believable to me—do I think it's possible?

4. **Commitment Worthy:** Am I fully committed to my vision? Do I own it? Do I embody it? Will I do whatever it takes?

Twenty-five years ago, I had a very clear vision of wanting to become a published author. In the last year, within nine months of each other, both my leadership book and my novel were published by mainstream publishers. That doesn't happen every day! My novel took twenty-five years to find a publisher; my leadership book took three months. I'm still pinching myself!

When I travelled to Scotland in 1995, I was very clear about the fact that I needed a life change and that, in some way, this trip would indeed be life changing. Taking the risk to go on my own to a place where I knew no one and driving a stick-shift on the left side of the road in a strange country led me to a village pub, playing darts, and meeting the love of my life—who became my husband a year later. It's a very cool story; maybe we'll risk trying to make it into a movie one day!

Creating my leadership programs digitally so people everywhere in the world can learn core leadership skills is perhaps the biggest professional vision I've had in the last few years. I didn't know how to make it happen; I just knew that I had to give it all I had. Talking with friends and colleagues led to finding partners who believed in me and the vision. We took a huge risk to trust our combined resources and talents so that we could create something substantial that makes us feel proud.

Then I risked doing a TEDx talk, then the books came out, then my AskRoxi radio show. Yes, sometimes it feels really scary, and sometimes it feels like magic; I believe each of us can make our own magic when we vision, take risks, and do the hard work.

It all starts by believing you are ENOUGH! And of course by reminding yourself, over and over again, "Nothing ventured, nothing gained!"

Roxi Bahar Hewertson is an author, speaker, teacher, and coach to leaders within higher education, business, and non-profits. Her acclaimed book, "Lead Like it Matters… Because it Does," provides leaders with a step-by-step practical roadmap to achieve great results. She is the CEO of Highland Consulting Group, Inc. and AskRoxi.com.

www.AskRoxi.com

HOW WOULD YOU LIKE YOUR COFFEE?

by Dr. Deborah J. Hrivnak

I t was a Thursday morning, six months ago, when my husband and I stopped by a local Starbucks. We had planned an extended weekend to visit our ten grandchildren and celebrate the second birthday of the youngest. As I stepped up to place my order, the barista smiled and told me he thought I was a famous celebrity, well known as an actress, television host, model, and author. I laughed hysterically at his kind words and anxiously shared his observation with my husband.

In a brief moment, I realized that instead of thanking the barista for his kind words, I had chosen to laugh aloud. Was it my insecure way of saying, "Are you kidding me, I am certainly not a model or actress? I am not a celebrity."

As we left the coffee shop with our drinks, I proudly told my husband that I could understand why the barista thought I was someone famous. I had on sunglasses that easily disguised who I really was, and my long, full hair was exceptionally beautiful that day. I could see why, even for a brief moment, he thought I was someone else... I admit that getting another star on my Gold Level Starbucks rewards was nice. It was even sweeter that someone actually thought I was a celebrity...a real rock star! At the same time, I realized this young man was being genuine.

He did not have to say anything to me at all other than to ask me what kind of coffee I wanted that morning. He had been nothing but authentic with me. Moreover, it made me wonder…

In that moment, the barista saw me as a celebrity, but unfortunately, in that same moment, I was not able to embrace his kind words. How would I excuse my dismissive laughter?

The barista did not know I could have several reasons for not feeling like a rock star. I mean, growing up poor to teenage parents, leaving a marriage and raising two boys alone, and the tremendous financial challenges that would ensue would affect me for years.

He did not know I had experienced harassment and bullying in the workplace, the stress of 80-hour weeks, and repeated job loss due to "restructuring." What would he have said to me if I had told him that I had just lost my closest friend the week before to cancer?

No, he would not know any of this, and so much more. He did not know the obstacles, the pain, and the struggles I had experienced for so many years. He did not even know that there were days when I felt the only comfort I could find was in the hot coffee drink he was responsible for making.

If we were to have a cup of coffee together, the barista would learn, however, the greatest obstacle before me was the diagnosis of a chronic health condition. He would also learn that this chronic health condition would change my life, and conquering it would become one of my greatest successes.

In November 2008, my family physician told me I had type 2 diabetes. The stress I had experienced in my work environment, the lack of exercise, poor eating habits, and my age had led to a condition I was already at high risk for. No Rewards Star for the poor decisions I had been making regarding my health.

I do not think the initial diagnosis scared me. I knew with proper diet and exercise, I would easily beat it. Then the anger, shock, denial, and fear set in as I found I was not able to manage my condition as I needed to. I cried a lot and experienced despair as I had never experienced before. I never blamed God; however, I realize I kept God very distant.

For thirty-four years, I had served students with special needs, assuring them the services they deserved to be successful. I also had become a certified life coach and spent decades studying personal growth and development –; supporting individuals to become more than they thought they could be, achieving goals, and seeing their dreams unfold. Now I found myself dying a slow death, and often times, not even caring. Never before had I experienced so much fear and anxiety regarding my future. I had to make some choices other than how to take my coffee.

When I changed my perspective, my life changed significantly for the better. I chose to see the last "restructuring" and subsequent job loss as a huge blessing. I also chose to see my diabetic condition as one of the greatest blessings I had been given.

My success came from getting clear on what I wanted: to be happy and healthy. I also discovered my why: because I have ten beautiful grandchildren, and I want to celebrate their birthdays for as long as I can. I took massive action—eating properly, working out for an hour a day, meditating, and fully enjoying my three- to four-mile walks every day.

Part of my journey was to recognize I could not do it alone, and partnering with God again was a priority. I also needed to consider creating more fun in my life, which I have successfully done throughout the past year. At any time, when things did not appear to be working, I changed my approach…small authentic actions.

Six years later (thirty-nine pounds lighter and with a normal hemoglobin A1C), I know I am nothing less than the celebrity the barista saw that day. Our challenges tell stories—stories of courage…stories of moving forward… stories of bravery…stories of vulnerability…stories of success.

Despite one's fears and the challenges and obstacles life brings, one can make the choice to show up and be real. Showing up, taking action, overcoming, persevering, changing and being greater than our obstacles are the most authentic things we can do. Enjoy your choices, in coffee and in life!

———————

Dr. Deborah Hrivnak is a certified coach, speaker, author, professor, and creator of *Get Off the Sidelines and Into the 'Game.'* Deborah works with small businesses, individuals, and teams on how to leverage their strengths for greater productivity, engagement, and profits. She also works with special needs students and their families.

www.MyCoachDeborah.com

CONFIDENCE, COURAGE, AND CARING—THE ADVENTURE STORY OF SUCCESS IN HELPING OTHERS

by John Hrivnak

A looming deadline faces a brand new board of directors wanting to open a community health center in rural Kansas. In three weeks, the clinic needs to have seen its first patient or lose federal funding. They have no location and call me to discuss my expertise in medical architecture.

Listening to their story, I courageously suggest that they don't need an architect (not the best marketing pitch). Instead, I write on the whiteboard a sequential list of what they need to accomplish before their deadline. It is not a small list—among the line items are filing for 501-C3, creating a business plan, hiring staff, writing job descriptions, recruiting a physician, writing/adopting protocols, acquiring equipment acquisition, accounting, creating charting and operational systems, and yes—some place to have the clinic. Shocked into reality, jaws dropping, they ask if I can help with that.

Confidently, I answer, "Yes," and the adventure begins. A common thread in my life, in terms of what drives me is the compelling desire to bring dignity to those who need it most, rises up with the "yes" before I consider fully what is before me. I just know that there are medically underserved people in this community who will stay that way if I don't do this—now. Driven by caring, I know that the courage and confidence will surface.

The adventure begins—and I love it!

While I may be a licensed architect and have an MBA in finance and have done commercial real estate, I am fully unqualified in any traditional sense to take on the role of co-founder of a federally funded medical clinic. I am, however, passionate about helping others and confident that in spite of never having done this before—it will be done—it will be done well—and it will be done within the incredibly short timeframe.

My goal was not to create a clinic for indigent care, but rather to create a clinic that would be the clinic of choice for anyone in the community in serving a broad spectrum of people. My drive was to convey dignity to the underserved—they deserve the best—the very same as anyone who can afford the care. So…the "design" of the clinic in all that it would do was to compete with the best in the area…and win.

As mentioned, I'd never recruited physicians before—talked to recruiters who wanted big dollars we didn't have. Creative problem solving: rural Kansas offers no mountains, oceans, or big city life to entice doctors—what we did have was hunting and fishing. Connecting the dots, I run ads in "Field & Stream" for doctors. It works. I learn that federally funded clinics get malpractice insurance paid for by the government. Connecting the dots—greatest malpractice insurance is OB/GYN—so we recruit that specialty, offer great service for less, and conquer that market in the region. Profitably. We are a not-for-profit being run like a business.

Believing that everyone has some God-given gift and a passion, I ask staff members what they would really like to do. One of them loves working with kids—we begin out-sourcing nurses to local schools, saving them money, profitably for us. Another loves reaching out to the community for flu shots—she is appointed "in charge" of that program with my full support. She builds that into a phenomenal success—and more profit and PR for the clinic. Still another has experience working with inmates. I talk to the sheriff and learn that the costs at the local jail for a medical encounter include paying for a police escort to the doctor. We set up a clinic in the jail—yes, I can do the architecture to create the exam room in an extra space they have—and we reduce their medical encounter costs by over half and still charge rates that are profitable to us.

This fledgling indigent care clinic in rural Kansas is, in year one, now the medical provider for the school system, the medical provider for the local jail, the clinic of choice for OB/GYN (we end up hiring our competitor), the "everywhere" flu shot provider, omnipresent on the radio with ads and interviews, I'm speaking at every fraternal organization in the area, and yes—we serve anyone, regardless of their ability to pay—with dignity.

You might imagine the waiting room in our new location—full of noisy kids while Mom and one of the kids is in an exam room, or at the W.I.C. (women, infants, and children nutrition) desk—these kids and others waiting deserve treatment with dignity, too. So, the Executive Director (me) sits down on the floor to play with the kids. A pharmaceutical rep shows up at the front desk demanding to see the executive director. The receptionist looks at me sitting on the floor wondering what to do and responds "he's busy." I stand, let the gentleman know that I'm the director and that, yes, I am busy with the kids. He can make an appointment at the desk. I return to play with the kids—letting them know that they matter; the theme of dignity continues to drive my out-of-the-box behavior.

Some of our funding comes through Medicare/Medicaid, and they pay slowly. My CFO and I travel to visit with them and negotiate a trade deal; we provide them with all invoicing in their format, one-click transfer to their software programs to make it easy and save time on their end, in trade for simultaneous electronic transfer of payment. Days receivable in that category goes to zero. Those who can't pay are offered a sliding fee schedule (dignity), and in one case, a trade for services to launder our providers' white lab coats (dignity).

Year one results: Fastest growing community health center in Kansas and most profitable not-for-profit (we put it into reserves, advertising, and bonuses for our enthusiastic staff).

The adventure continues as I seek to confidently, courageously bring dignity to our clients, driven by caring.

———————

John Hrivnak, AIA, MBA, NCARB, LEED AP, ArCH, is a professional architect, professor, consultant and president of Hrivnak Associates, Ltd. John provides creative solutions and program management for capital improvement programs nationwide.

www.HrivnakAssociates.com

FREE FALLING

by Deborah Kagan

I thought for sure I'd lost my mind as I lay prostrate, face down on my kitchen floor. It was 1997. A lovely summer day in West Hollywood, California. The birds were singing, the sun was shining, and everything seemed to click along normally...except in my kitchen.

Moments prior I had been standing in my robe making a tea latte. Next thing I know, I got bitch-slapped *really, really hard* on the back of my neck. So hard I wound up on the floor. That might all make sense if there was an actual other person in my apartment. Alas, just me. Here's where it gets even more "Twilight Zone-y." I heard whispering. Like the whispers in the TV from "Poltergeist." They don't make sense at first. It's when you shout back at them saying, *WHAT?! I hear you. But what-are-you-saying?!* That's when they press pause on the static button, part the energy field and say three words in one very eerie, albeit clear voice: Light. Love. Truth. And whoosh. Whatever was there exited the building like it was late for lunch with a lover.

That shove from above, as I've come to call it, changed my life. I had been teetering with keeping my career in the film business, you know, to have something to fall back on, while at the same time I was starting a Feng Shui consulting business.

As much as I tried to ignore the shove for a few days, it lingered. I could feel it leaning on me in the shower. I could feel it sitting shotgun in my car

96

giving me googly eyes. I could feel it spooning with me in bed. Until I finally couldn't ignore it anymore.

Fine! I huffed. What now?

Before I knew it, I found myself walking into the Bodhi Tree Bookstore, THE new age mecca in Los Angeles. I loved wandering around in there. Fabulous people watching. A bazillion books to peruse. Groovy crystal-y things to ogle.

Wandering towards the astrology aisle, a pretty blonde, cut straight from a JC Penny catalog, sat pouring over the book "Lovesigns," while a 40-something soccer mom stood wistfully reading pages from a Rumi poetry book.

I found myself in the symbols/symbolism section. A thin, orange book literally fell off the shelf by my feet. Being on this quest to pay attention to these new, persistent messages, I picked up the book and read the title, "The Book of Signs" (how's that for on the nose?). I flipped through the first few pages, and there they were. Triangles. Big deal you might be thinking. A geometric symbol used in math and science. Whoopdeedo. Here's where it gets freaky. $\triangle$ represents Light. The masculine. ∇ represents Truth. The feminine. Put the two of them together, and you get Love. A beautiful union of the masculine and feminine. The complete picture of what's so in the universe, and the message that had originally knocked me down. That's when I knew synchronicity exists. For reals.

Some people get cancer. Some car accidents. Some lose a loved one. I got the psychic slap to fall down in order to soar. I had no idea exactly how it would go. What I did know was to pay closer attention to the whispers, let instincts be the guide, see where it leads, and allow my life to change. What you are meant to learn and experience falls into your life, the question is how to take the opportunity and recalibrate.

Since that oh-so-wild morning in my sweet Spanish bungalow of an apartment, I have built a thriving Feng Shui consulting business working in private homes, corporate offices, Hollywood film sets, hotels, and even a casino in Vegas. Atma Jewels, a complimentary product line, was birthed in 2000, making headlines in numerous publications, and was featured in a celebrity-gifting suite.

The year 2008 ushered in the next big shove from above. This time it was way friendlier. I was in New Orleans at the Superdome for the tenth anniversary of VDAY, a global organization dedicated to ending violence against women. I wasn't even three feet inside when the voice from above fell into my brain.

"Hey, Deborah. It's time to get up off your ass and do the work with women."

I could feel my body falling forward into the YES of the message, which is a distinctly different feeling than tipping back into a NO.

"I don't know what you want me to do. But I'm listening," I replied.

Nearly six years later, from the humble beginnings of hosting women's circles in my living room to stages speaking to as many as a thousand at a time, I've had the pleasure of working with over 10,000 women, in person or online, helping them rock their mojo. Plus, I've had the honor of producing two events featuring Calista Flockhart, Rosario Dawson, Dylan McDermott, Christine Lahti, and others where we raised money and awareness for VDAY, a cause close to my heart.

Some people's RockStar moment hits them bluntly over the head. For most of us, it's much more subtle. It's an idea or thought or feeling that haunts you and lingers. Start paying attention to that and take actions congruent with the message.

My entrée to being an entrepreneur came from a psychic bitch-slap to the neck. Normal? I'd say not. Fits the trend for my life, though, as I've never been much of a conventional one. Which works to my benefit as an entrepreneur. Because when you're out to blaze a trail, make a mark, or share your gift with the world, it's better if you can play on the edge.

And hey, when we have the pleasure to meet, remind me to show you how I made an indelible mark to remember that moment, the one that allowed me to get up off the floor and create a life worth living.

———————

Deborah Kagan helps women rock their mojo. She is the creator of the Rock Your Mojo™ programs and the author of "Find Your ME Spot: 52 Ways to Reclaim Your Confidence, Feel Good in Your Own Skin and Live a Turned On Life."

For all things mojolicious, check out www.deborah-kagan.com.

FAMILY TIES

by Melody Keymer Harper

F amily! As far back as I can remember, my parents said there was nothing more important in life than family. "People come and go, but your family will always be there for you." Mom and Dad also stressed the importance of getting a college degree and developing a strong Christian faith. To this day, some sixty years later, family is still the most important thing to me, as is education and my faith in God.

What I am most proud of and feel is the greatest success in my life is having raised my three incredible, productive, and caring children. They all have been greatly influenced by the values that were given to me and that I have tried to impart to them. All three have college degrees, wonderful spouses, and two adorable children, blessing me with a total of six grandchildren.

As is with my siblings and their families, my three children, Greg, Lisa, and Tracy, are the best of friends. They truly value the special relationship and time they have together. A close relationship is as important to them as it is to my sisters and brother through raising their children around their cousins and extended family.

I was raised in a small, middle class community in San Gabriel, California, where I attended elementary school, high school, and the local college. I grew up in a family of six: my mom, dad, older sister, older brother, twin sister, and me. We did pretty much everything together. We ate together, played games, went on vacations, celebrated special occasions, and attended church every

Sunday. Friday nights were Family Nights around our house. We all cuddled in front of the TV in our pajamas and ate pizza, chips and dips, brownies, and ice cream sodas as we watched a family-friendly movie.

Later I married my college sweetheart, and within the next three years gave birth to my precious baby boy and two beautiful baby girls, whom have meant more to me than anything I could have ever imagined. Unfortunately, our marriage did not survive, leaving me with my three children, ages 5 months, 1 year, and 2 years old, and the challenges of raising them on my own.

My goal was to be the best mother I could be and to instill in my children those important family values my parents had instilled in me. Fortunately, my children's father and I have maintained a healthy, respectful relationship for the benefit of our children. To this day, we have remained close friends. My children have expressed their appreciation of the relationship. Many of their friends have commented on how fortunate they are to have divorced parents who act so civilly toward each other. Many of them have suffered through painfully destructive family divorces.

As a single parent, I wanted to share the same family values and memories with my children as I had growing up. Therefore, we ate together, played games, went on family vacations, celebrated special occasions, and attended church on Sundays, just as I had done. The Friday Family Night tradition was continued.

My sisters, brother and I were given numerous opportunities to participate in sports, extra-curricular activities, community outreaches, and church youth group programs, which I provided for my children as well. Our parents supported us in whatever we did, as I did for my children.

On my own, and responsible for guiding my three children's lives, I decided to take charge of my life and finish what I had started so many years ago with my education. My mom's words still rang in my ears: "There is just one thing I would like to see before I die—that you finish your college education and get a degree like the rest of the family."

Though I know my mother loved me dearly, I realize now her words were unintentionally hurtful and supposed to be a motivational tactic. All it did at that time was make me feel inadequate. However, as I was raising my children, my mother gave me some insightful information when she said, "How can you expect your children to sense the importance of getting a higher education if you have not accomplished it yourself?"

It was a given family expectation that college followed high school. It was just a matter of deciding which college to attend. I wanted to nurture that educational expectation in my three children in order for them to have more opportunities in their lives to become self-sufficient and contributing adults. I became driven to be the best role model possible for them—thus, back to college again to complete what I had begun years before.

Two years later, I completed my Bachelor of Arts degree in Psychology. What a monumental day! Graduation day was a grand celebration, with family watching as I accepted my long-awaited diploma. I had no idea what an impact that little paper showing I had crossed the finish line would have on me. All the effort, time, money, and sacrifice I had made going back to college turned out to be one of the best decisions I had ever made. It changed my thinking forever and reinforced the empowerment of education.

This most meaningful benchmark of my life was succeeded by my three children receiving their college degrees. Eventually, I went on to receive two teaching credentials and a master's degree. Although I felt a sense of accomplishment from my master's degree and credentials, nothing could compare to the feeling of confidence and self-worth receiving my bachelor's degree had given me. It opened my eyes to the awareness of possibilities of what is really available when you set goals and apply yourself.

I am forever thankful for the family values my parents instilled in me for strong family relationships, education, and a Christian faith. This has enabled me to not only raise three healthy children, all thriving and successful in their careers and raising their own families with the strength of those same family values, it has also provided me the tools to effectively make a difference in other people's lives.

––––––––––

Melody Keymer Harper is a professional speaker, author, radio host, consultant, and creator of Melody Keymer Harper's Ignite Your Inner Power. Melody speaks to entrepreneurs, parents, churches, and colleges on how to get the winning results you want on stage, your education, your career, and your life.

www.melodykeymerharper.com

Kopf Brothers Crested Butte to Aspen Ski Race

by Chris Kopf

The Elk Mountain Grand Traverse is an annual endurance ski race starting in Crested Butte, Colorado, at midnight, finishing in Aspen the next day. In this extreme endurance event, racers will travel 40+ miles, climb more than 7,800 vertical feet, and navigate in a self-supported backcountry race that tests them physically and mentally. To maintain safety in the backcountry, racers compete in teams of two and are required to carry mandatory gear. Held annually since 1998, it has earned a reputation as a true test of toughness for elite local, national, and international athletes.

I moved my family from Dallas to Crested Butte in 2009, and shortly thereafter my brother and I decided we wanted to compete in the Grand Traverse. Our team name was "Kopf Brothers"—Chris Kopf & Rick Kopf. In comparison to the other racers, we were the old guy rookie team (I was 50 and Rick was 56). Our stated goals were

1. Do not die.
2. Finish.
3. Don't be last.

Of course our wives and friends said we were nuts.

We did not know what we did not know. There were hundreds of details and questions about equipment, navigation, and safety, but weighing heaviest on our minds was whether a prolonged stop would introduce hypothermia and frostbite? As one advisor told us, "You really don't understand this race until you finish."

We had completed the Texas Water Safari, which was a 260-mile canoe race, but this was much different given the risk of avalanche danger and extreme cold. We are expert downhill skiers but had very little backcountry skiing and winter survival experience. The fear of the unknown was a strong motivator, and we knew that to support each other and finish we needed to be in great physical condition. We trained on average 90 minutes per day, six days per week for nearly, five months prior to the race. My training was mostly solo uphill climbing on skis in the dark. Rick lived and trained mainly in Dallas—mostly on a stair machine and on roller skis (yes, roller skis).

On race day there was a storm, which increased the avalanche danger at Death Pass and Star Pass. We said a brief prayer prior to the race start. The gun sounded at midnight, and we were off…

We climbed up and over Mt. Crested Butte before starting the long march up Brush Creek toward Star Pass. If we did not make it to Star Pass by 8 a.m., we would be turned around.

Arrival, Death Pass: 3 a.m. I had a huge blister on my left heel; I stopped and used duct tape as a bandage—a mistake because soon I had a wad of duct tape rubbing against the blister.

Death Pass is aptly named, because there is a traverse across a very steep avalanche slide area with ice chunks, trees, and rocks above a cliff and rushing icy water below.

Checkpoint two is the Friends Hut, and when we arrived at 6:15 a.m. our fingers and toes were frozen. Our vision of a warm friendly checkpoint with a hut to rest in quickly vanished: There was no hut, it was cold, and we were exposed to high winds. With no reason to stay and shiver, we pushed on. The climb was steep and endless.

Life Lesson: The top is only a place from which you can see the next peak.

At one point, we saw that a racer had slid fifty yards below the traverse line and was struggling to climb back up. To avoid the same fate, we searched for the smallest cuts in the ice to hold the edge of our skis.

Star Pass summit: 7:15 a.m. The beautiful sunrise was worth the effort. We were less than half way, but we would not be turned back!

Skiing down the steep backside of Star Pass through deep snow was very difficult on skinny skis with heavy packs. We fell multiple times, and it took great effort to get back up.

At the Taylor Pass checkpoint, we enthusiastically asked the race officials, "which way down?" They held back their laughter and pointed to the top of the next peak and said: "Sorry, you still have to climb to the top of that peak…but then it is all downhill from there."

Life Lesson: It is never "all downhill from there."

At the Barnard Hut checkpoint, there was a mandatory rest and inspection by a doctor. The blister on my heel was screaming, but I chose not to mention it for fear I would be forced to withdraw. We were given hot soup, warm Gu, and cold pizza.

We were told we had seven "quick and flat" miles to the Aspen Sun deck. Instead, it was brutally long, constantly up hill, and mentally tiring. We motivated each other to keep pushing.

We envisioned the Sun Deck as a mountain restaurant crowded with well-wishers, music, and cheering… NOT! There were three race officials with clipboards.

The final 3,300 feet from the Sun Deck to the base area was downhill, but hard, as our packs were heavy and our legs were spent.

We stopped at the top of the last hill and now looked down at the finish. We had made it! There was a crowd, there was cheering, and they announced our names over the loudspeaker, "Here come the Kopf Brothers!"

After five months of preparation and very hard training, we had done it—we had arrived at the finish! The weight of the moment hit us. We shed tears of joy.

Rick looked at me and said: "I couldn't have done it without you!" Looking back, I replied: "I wouldn't have done it without you!"

Our official time was 15 hours, 4 minutes, and 25 seconds. We are among an elite group who has finished.

We lacked knowledge and experience, but we succeeded because we had the will. We put a plan in place, we did not quit, and we achieved our goal.

Chris Kopf is a Top Real Estate Agent in the resort town of Crested Butte Colorado. Chris is a professional speaker, author, radio host, and creator of The Resort Real Estate Agent System for Success—How to Become a Top Real Estate Agent in Your Resort Market. Chris teaches quick and easy tips to help agents transform their real estate business—and their lives!

www.ResortRealEstateCoach.com

AND THE EMMY GOES TO...
CHANGE OF HEART

by Janie Lidey

I used to wonder what Einstein meant when he said, "Imagination is more important than knowledge." I was a pretty bright kid and got good grades in school, but I was also the kid that would stare endlessly out the window of my classroom, seemingly lost in my imagination. It wasn't until I became a teacher and taught for many years that I began to realize the significance of Einstein's message, and its power to help manifest our dreams.

As a nine year old, my imagination began to run wild when I saw the new Coke commercial on TV that featured the song *I'd like To Teach the World to Sing*. It was the most beautiful advertisement I'd ever seen, showing people from many cultures sharing a song, a Coke, and a message about spreading peace, love, and happiness across the land. When I saw that commercial, something happened inside of me that made me feel like, someday, I would write a song like that and be part of a similar message. I wasn't a musician yet but I am convinced that this commercial was a big part of what sparked my desire to start playing the guitar a few years later. Hearing that one special song was enough to stir something in my imagination that would shape my future with more certainty than any knowledge ever could have.

Fast forward more than three decades, and you can find a commercial on the NBC TV affiliate in Alaska that is reminiscent of that famous Coca Cola commercial from the seventies. It is a beautiful advertisement showing people from many cultures sharing a song and a message about spreading peace, love, and happiness across the land. The song is called *Change of Heart* and was written by me, Janie Lidey. That Coke advertisement, and its effect on my imagination, sparked more than just a new song and television commercial. After high school, I attended college, where I got my degree in Music Education, and I really was teaching the world to sing in perfect harmony.

Twenty years into my teaching career, I was asked to write a song for a campaign on tolerance. I was the choir director at East Anchorage High School and had been known to perform some of my original music with my choirs. Some members of our community had decided to create a series of public service announcements for an anti-hate campaign, and they invited me to compose a song to help promote their message. After writing the song, I would teach it to my choir, and one of the local television stations would help create a video that would air for thirty seconds and run for three months on our NBC affiliate. This was the commercial that I had imagined in my youth! My dream of spreading peace, love, and happiness through the magic of a song was coming true, and to make things even more magical, I ended up winning an Emmy award in the category of musical composer for the song that I wrote.

So how did I get the Emmy nomination? There is an award given in Alaska television called the Goldie Award, which honors the very best of broadcasting in Alaska. *Change of Heart* won two of those Goldies—one for Service to Community and one for Public Service Announcement. Once you have won a Goldie, you can be nominated for an Emmy, which is what happened to me!

Winning an Emmy was a dream come true, but aside from the huge personal growth and success I was experiencing, I began noticing the incredible influence it was having on my students. Suddenly there was a new respect for the level of excellence we were striving for and achieving together in the East High Fine Arts Department! My students were rising up, becoming more successful in all areas of their lives. Success begets success, and what I started hearing from other teachers was that my kids were doing better in all of their classes because of what was happening to them in mine! Kids were walking the talk of this new message about tolerance in our community, and it was raising them up to higher standards in every aspect of their lives.

We all define success in different ways. As a musician, you are definitely considered a Rock Star if you win an Emmy or a Grammy! And if you listen closely to the acceptance speeches given at those ceremonies, you will almost always hear thanks being given to God, parents, teachers, children, friends, etc. Success would mean nothing if there were no one to share it with. And I have come to realize that if I lived alone on this planet, there would be no one to inspire an Emmy-award-winning song. The things I write about would not come from a heart untouched by love, so while I am the one who got to accept the award, and I am the one who gets to keep it on my piano, my Emmy really goes to…all of the people who have touched my heart.

During the years that followed this magical event in my life, I began to feel a shift in my purpose. Something kept telling me to step out of the comfort of one classroom and make the world my classroom. Seeing what this song and its message had done for my community made me wonder what kind of impact I could have on a global level. I truly wanted to raise the vibration of love on our planet, and my Emmy had given me the confidence to take a leap of faith. I retired early from teaching, shifting my purpose to raising the vibration on our beautiful earth and bringing her back into balance through the magic of a song.

Oh, and that little thirty-second PSA that was supposed to air for three months became a ninety-second PSA that has been on air changing hearts for over ten years!

Janie Lidey is an Emmy award winning songwriter, professional speaker, author, and recording artist. Janie speaks and sings at women's conferences, personal growth seminars, music festivals, and more on how to raise your vibration and attract blessings and miracles every day.

www.janielidey.com

I BELIEVE EVERYONE SHOULD BE A REAL ESTATE INVESTOR

by Steve Love

Today, things are good for me, I mean really, really good!
We have two great kids, who we adore.
I have the time and financial freedom to do what I really love to do. For me, that's working my business while helping others, plus spending lots of time playing.

Believe me, things were not always as they are today. I was broke, divorced, and miserable. The cat was my only joy in life. Then I discovered how to invest in real estate, and that changed everything for me. If you'd like to learn more about what happened, read on...

First, let me describe my life today. Then I'll get into how it really was and what changed it all. As stated above, much of my life today consists of playing (fun and leisure stuff).

Playing for me consists of many activities. These include monthly fishing trips, several ocean cruises per year of one to two weeks, frequent live rock and roll concerts (I love Neil Young, Bruce Springsteen, the Rolling Stones, and Fleetwood Mac), a couple trips monthly to The Magic Castle (a private magic club where I'm a member), and two professional or personal development seminars every month (either in real estate or personal growth seminars like with Tony Robbins or Jack Canfield, etc.).

We love live theater and attend several plays per year, attend movies weekly, occasional comedy shows (I love Jeff Dunham, Bette Midler, and even Daniel Tosh), and our family enjoys going to see local professional sports teams. My kids are athletes, so I go to their football, basketball, baseball, water polo, and hockey games—one of my most fulfilling parental activities. I love watching my favorite shows on TV with my wife. We also love massages, dining out at least a couple times per week, and traveling through the state (especially to Yosemite) or all over the globe.

How about my biggest blessing of all: having the **time** to do what I want, with whom I want, whenever I want. I see so many people who have to work 40+ hours per week, commute in traffic, sometimes work two jobs, and are too exhausted to enjoy life. Money is important, very important. But TIME, I've realized, is even more valuable. Since I'm not struggling 24/7 to survive, I can help others. I give back and teach others how to live life more abundantly. This privilege I don't take lightly.

It wasn't always this way! No, there were hard times. I was recently divorced, had no money, no real job, no girlfriend, no prospects for the future, and was miserable. Then I discovered real estate investing.

I learned that buying houses didn't require capital (good, because I had none!), credit, or even much time. It does require specialized knowledge. I learned how by attending seminars. I took all I could, and soon my whole attitude and outlook for the future changed. I purchased my first property and haven't looked back since.

I then met the girl of my dreams, Robyn. There is not a more supportive or wonderful girl for me. I took her for a trip to Yosemite, asked her to marry me, we got married (by my spiritual teacher, Amma), and had our first child two years later.

We started buying more properties until we were asked by one of the top real estate trainers in the country to start our own REIA (Real Estate Investors Association) in Los Angeles. Although not really a profitable endeavor, it has been the most satisfying thing I've ever done. This is where most of my work hours are spent. It allows me to "give back" to others wanting to improve their lives, it has allowed me to get to know most of the great real estate trainers/ investors out there, and it has even produced deals for us from our attendees. To learn more about where and when we meet, who the next trainer is, etc., go to www.prosperitythroughrealestate.com.

There are two main categories of investing: The Buy/Sell and the Buy/ Hold businesses. One produces big checks, the other passive monthly income. We do both.

How many houses do you need? For most of us, just 10–15 free and clear (no debt on the property) houses are all you need. That's enough to live the lifestyle and have the freedom desired. If not, buy a few more houses. How long will it take? We know investors who buy a house a week or more.

Suffice it to say that real estate changed my life, it has changed countless others' lives, and I know it can change yours, too. It will also take some ACTION on your part, but nothing that you cannot do.

Investing in real estate is not a "get rich quick" scheme. Although it's true that the richest people I know got that way via real estate, it usually didn't happen overnight. For most, it's a gradual process.

So is my life now 100 percent bliss? Heck no! We still have problems: Our new puppy is not yet house trained (yuck!), my fishing trip just got cancelled, traffic in Los Angeles sucks, I'm usually irritated with Congress and the people in Washington D.C., computers don't like me, and teenagers are, well, teenagers!

Life isn't all roses, but I am aware of my many blessings, how much life has changed since the "dark times," and how fortunate I am compared to life before real estate investing and compared to so many peoples' lives today.

If you're going through a dark period or you'd just like a little (or a lot) more money in your life, let real estate help you out, too! I'm convinced that anyone who wants to do this can learn to invest. No, money cannot solve all problems, but it can make your problems easier to cope with. As mentioned earlier, I'd be glad to help you.

––––––––––

Steve Love is a successful real estate investor, broker, and trainer. He is the Co-Executive Director of Prosperity Through Real Estate, an educational real estate investors club in Los Angeles. He speaks on cruise ships throughout the world and is the author or co-author of several real estate books.

www.prosperitythroughrealestate.com

NOT ONLY SURVIVING, BUT THRIVING...

by Carey McLean

I could never have imagined what it feels like to be told that you are about to start the fight of your life, and cancer is the opponent. After hearing those three words from my breast surgeon on the phone, "They found cancer," my life changed forever, as well as the lives of the people around me. My hope is that my story impacts others and encourages them to be their best self and to always fight a good fight. You never know when you're going to need it.

On December 20, 2014, I was excited as ever to be going home to Minnesota for a two-week holiday visit. I took a red-eye from Sacramento that was to land in Minneapolis at 5:30 a.m. After I landed, I went to the nearest Orangetheory Fitness Studio in Apple Valley to make my 8:15 a.m. workout, as an OTFer groupie would.

Later that day, I had a conversation with my Aunt Deb that would change my life forever. I owe my life, and this year's outcome, to her for that one little conversation. And I can never thank my family and friends enough for all their support and love that I received this year. I do believe that things happen for a reason, no matter how good or bad we perceive them to be.

While I was home, I told my mom, "I think I found something." It felt like a mini golf ball in my right breast, and I could move it a little by grabbing onto it with my thumb and index finger.

Every day, for two weeks, I knew it was there, kept checking it…but planned on it being nothing. I made a decision right then that I would not spend energy on something that I could not control. The only thing I could control was how I lived my life going forward.

Immediately after returning home to Sacramento, I saw my family doctor. That led to a mammogram and ultrasound. Doctors told me that it was probably benign because the tumor did not seem to have the characteristics of cancer. Either way, the lump was bothering me, and I wanted it removed.

I was referred to a breast surgeon to help me through this journey. My first surgery date was set for January 28. The fine needle aspiration before surgery did not indicate cancer either, so my doctor proceeded to take out the tumor.

In January 2014, I was blessed to be able to attend Maryann Ehmann's "Create Your Magnificent Life" at Coronado Beach. After going to this amazing three-day event, my goal for 2014 was to talk with God on a regular basis and journal what I heard. This became something that I would do in order to gain clarity and guidance in my life.

About two days before my first scheduled surgery, I wrote the following journal entry:

Monday, January 26, 2015
Dear God,
Why am I so strong and able to handle this? (As I am driving to work, crying)

Dear Carey,
Because I made you that way.

After I heard those words in my head, my tears immediately stopped. I felt a kind of peace that couldn't be ignored. I knew I was going to be okay. With every decision I made in 2015, I waited for that same feeling and accepted it. My only job was to research, evaluate, make a decision, and move on. Very similar to what I do in business.

The morning of the lumpectomy, which would tell me if it was cancerous or not, I made the following journal entry:

Wednesday, January 28, 2015
Dear God,
*   Why am I able to get through this surgery and move on with my everyday life as if it was just a bump in the road?*

Dear Carey,
*   It is just a bump… A little one at that:). You will recover amazingly fast and be back golfing, working out, and enjoying life in no time!*

After surgery, I was led to believe that the lump was removed and that it was benign. My doctor told me the following: Fibroadenoma of the breast is a benign tumor. Benign tumor means it is not caused by cancer.

I thought I was in the clear and was so grateful that it was benign and would not affect me further. About a week later, I got a phone call while sitting in the San Diego airport on my way to Baltimore for a software developer event. As I talked to my doctor on the phone, I heard him say, "They found cancer." Tears rolled down my face immediately as I sat in the waiting area to board my flight.

I made the following journal after I got the news:

Thursday, February 5, 2015
Dear God,
*   Why am I strong enough and courageous enough to make it through this?*

Dear Carey,
*   Because I made you that way and you never back down from a challenge.*
*   There's some connected reason why you are taking this path. Find it and meet it with the strength and courage I have gifted you with and that you use so well.*
*   You have so many people that love you and support you every step of the way. Utilize their positive energy as you often do.*

On February 5, 2015, at age 38, I was diagnosed with breast cancer. I made a decision early on that I would not change events on my calendar if I could help it. This included my business and golf events that I loved so much. Eight weeks after my bilateral mastectomy on my birthday, I won my Chapter Championship and advanced to semi-finals.

On August 1, eleven days after my third chemo treatment, I won semi-finals and advanced to finals. I played both days at the EWGA finals in Palm Springs, California, ten weeks after my final chemo treatment. I didn't win, but I had a blast, and I got to show up. Surviving. And thriving.

―――――――

Carey McLean is The App Chicks' creator, a technical guru, and a designer. Carey is goal oriented, queen of trouble-shooting, gets the job done efficiently, and is committed to serving success to her customers. As the lead App Chick, her cutting-edge ideas become reality for her clients who, incidentally, are never disappointed.

www.TheAppChicks.com

LEARNING TO FLOW
LIKE A BLACK BELT

by Melodee Meyer

I was on top of the world. After years of hard work, I finally had the dream job, at the dream company, creating my dream life. Little did I know that I was about to be abruptly awakened...

A couple years before, in 1998, my family and I were enjoying a happy, low-stress lifestyle on the island of Oahu. We didn't have a lot of money, but we loved running our martial arts business together. One day I got a job offer to work with a growing online adventure travel company in California. Wow—what an amazing opportunity to become part of the Internet boom!

So we packed up the kids and the dog, shut down our business in Hawaii and moved to the mainland to start our new adventure. I worked like crazy for the new company, and eventually, all the hard work paid off. By the year 2000, I was president of the world's largest online adventure travel club, I was directing the first adventure travel reality TV show at exotic locations around the world, and was on track to take our company public and become a gazzillionaire...

Life was grand, and I was on top of the world! I was finally going to have the money and lifestyle I had always wanted.

And then I woke up to a loud "POP"...the sound of the dot-com bubble bursting.

I wasn't too worried at first because we had already secured funding, and our business seemed stable enough. However, when our venture capitalist (the person funding our company) had a sudden heart attack and died, we began to freefall. Scrambling to raise new money to support the vision took me away from the core business, and by the time 9/11 struck, it was all over but the crying.

And there was lots of crying.

I had to let go of over 40 employees and a couple dozen more contractors. I had to close up our beautiful offices overlooking the La Jolla cove. I had to move everything into my living room and personally take on the company duties from there because I was determined to keep it going. I believed in this company with my whole heart, and I had shareholders that I was responsible to.

For almost two years, I continued to work the business out of my house, out of my own pocket and into a very deep hole of debt and depression. I was borrowing money to pay the rent and buy basic groceries. My health was deteriorating dramatically. I was in big trouble, but I didn't know how to stop, even though nothing was working. I had lost touch with myself, and I couldn't see straight.

One day, standing in the middle of the City College campus in Santa Barbara while my son was enrolling in classes, I looked around and had a moment of clarity. It was time to get grounded and to go back to my roots, my roots in the martial arts.

For me, martial arts had been more than exercise or self-defense. Martial arts had been a way of life, a philosophy, a value framework from which to live in the world. But I had lost sight of those values while building my "empire" and then got busy just trying to survive.

Hitting rock bottom provided me the opportunity to reinvent myself. I chose to return to the principles of martial arts and apply them to my business (and my life), which is what ultimately moved me from struggle to success.

One of the governing principles of martial arts is "Flow." "Flow" refers to the movement of energy. As martial artists, we train in cooperation with this energy so that movement requires less effort. We work with the energy instead of against it—my opponent becomes my partner. For instance, if a punch is being thrown at me, I train to move with that punch, in fact, to join with the energy of the punch and redirect it to where I want it to go. This is the opposite of attempting to stop the punch with brute force, which is virtually impossible.

I was ready to be back in the "Flow" of life. The forces I imagined against me were my allies, and I was ready to start working with them, instead of against them.

Within weeks, my family and I moved to Santa Barbara with a plan to open a dojo. The obstacles appeared insurmountable. We had no money. We were $200,000 in debt, had zero credit, and knew no one in a city that was already saturated with competition.

We took on another principle of martial arts, "Commitment." Against all logic, we made the "Commitment" to enroll 100 students in the first 90 days. This was not a goal, it was a "Commitment." Of course, there was the added incentive of not having a Plan B, so if we did not reach that number, we were on the streets. Period.

Looking back, it was the best of times. We were in the "Flow." We fulfilled our "Commitment" and went on to build a million dollar business that has won Best Martial Arts Studio in Santa Barbara for the last twelve years in a row and national recognition as USA Martial Arts School of the Year, 2013.

More importantly, our business serves our community and continues to transform the lives of thousands of students by providing education for the mind, body, and spirit. Thanks to the power of MasterMind, strategic team building, and the Internet, my work has now expanded to a global audience.

Being an entrepreneur has its challenges, but we all can choose to join in the power of "Flow" and train to redirect negative energy into positive results. And we can make a "Commitment" to actions that will ensure our success so that we can each live the life of our dreams.

––––––––––––

Melodee Meyer is an inspirational speaker, host of Radio Blab, and founder of Black Belt Life Academy. Master Mel puts the "POW" in empowerment by using martial arts principles and spiritual psychology to coach leaders, organizations, and entrepreneurs so they can become black belts in their businesses and their lives.

www.MasterMel.com

IBS—I'VE BEEN SILENT

by Karen O'Connor

I t all began that summer of 1975. I was 16. I hated my body—how it looked and how it felt. I remember gaining thirty pounds in less than three months, going from a petite size three to a size ten and then eventually fourteen. I wore hand-me-downs from my older brothers because they were baggy and hid my weight and bloated stomach.

I would skip breakfast in the mornings, as it no longer settled well in my gut. Wanting to lose weight, I would no longer eat from the school cafeteria. My first menstrual cycle lasted for months. I remember being told that stress and anxiety can affect your period. I underwent hormone injections to regulate my periods.

I remember being constipated all the time, my stomach bloated, and the extreme cramping and pain. The doctor told my mother it was all in my head and that "I was just acting out." He later accused me of lying when he said I missed an appointment. I remember how unhappy and miserable I was in high school and all throughout college. Was the doctor right? Was this all in my head?

I was not much better by the age of 20. At the urging of a friend, I went to see her gynecologist about my stomach pain. Within two weeks I had surgery to remove a benign ovarian cyst the size of a grapefruit. While still recovering from the surgery a month later, my stomach began to swell, as if someone

119

was pumping air into my gut. The pressure on my spine was so great I would double over in pain.

I phoned the doctor's office crying and pleading with the nurse to talk to the doctor. The Doc listening, but not hearing, arrogantly dismissed my concerns, telling me it was just "gas." As I hung up the phone, I felt embarrassed, ashamed for "complaining." Were my problems real? Was the pain really that bad?

Several years later and paranoid about the side effects of taking too many laxatives for constipation, I made an appointment to see a doctor. Some new tests were ordered. I was hopeful and at the same time feeling spiteful because I really wanted to be vindicated for all those years of feeling bad.

The results came back negative for any real problems. Informed that I could have a spastic colon, the doctor told me the same thing I had been hearing all my life. "Watch what you eat and increase your fiber."

Beaten down again, I questioned whether my pain, discomfort, and constipation were really that bad. If the doctors didn't think so, then I must be exaggerating. Was I a hypochondriac? Am I neurotic?

Many years later, during a routine visit to new gynecologist I casually mentioned my chronic constipation and stomach pain. I was caught off guard when I heard the words "Irritable Bowel Syndrome… IBS."

Finally, it was real. For so many years I had often fantasized about having a disease just to feel compassion and be understood. If there was something really wrong with my gut, there would be a diagnosis, a treatment plan, and then a cure.

But this is where my hope was crushed. You see, IBS is a "catch all" diagnosis characterized by a group of symptoms: recurring abdominal pain, cramping, bloating, and altered bowel habits (diarrhea and/or constipation). It is a functional disorder in which the intestines do not behave normally. It is not life threatening but often a long-term condition.

There is no organic cause and therefore no cure. IBS is still not well understood by medical science and by most doctors. Therefore, treatments and preventive measures are not well defined.

Depression and anxiety often co-exist with IBS and often doctors dismiss these symptoms as "all in your head." After thirty years of suffering, this was all I got.

It has been almost five years since I said, "no more." I was tired, exhausted, and fed-up with self-pity. I began researching everything I could find on the topic, including visiting chat rooms and reading books.

I experimented with new diets and foods, exercises (Tai Chi, Pilates, and Yoga), self-hypnosis, and meditation. What I discovered was that yoga eased my pain and helped alleviate the gas and bloating and that swimming was soothing to my stomach and allowed me time to think and relax.

Today I feel paroled from the "life sentence" of IBS. My gut is much happier, although I fight a constant battle with constipation. I am no longer embarrassed and ashamed of having a bowel disorder.

The doctors I had consulted with were probably just as frustrated as I was, unable to diagnosis and offer any treatment. I know now that it takes a collaborative effort from both patient and doctor. But ultimately, it is the patient's responsibility to be proactive, to ask questions, to not accept the status quo. I was silent—I did not speak up.

A funny thing about our guts is that researchers are now calling it our "second brain." It is able to communicate with the brain yet act independently to influence our behaviors, moods, how we think, learn, and remember.

Understanding this could mean new therapies and treatments for IBS as well as for many other illnesses, such as diabetes and obesity. I know now there is hope for some fifty million Americans with IBS, just like me. Could this be my mission, my purpose to help others overcome IBS? To be an advocate of good health?

Just today, under the darkness of morning, I swam laps in the soothing waters of a natural hot spring pool. I reflected back on the greatest decision of my life thirty-four years ago to run away and become a ski bum in Colorado. I know now, my gut, whether intuition or intelligence, led me here. I just needed to listen and trust myself. I am blessed with good health and my unique second brain. No longer silent, but heard!

———————

Karen O'Connor is a back office specialist, investor, real estate broker, author, and educator. Karen works with small business owners building back office systems. Karen's new platform, BackOfficeTips.com provides tips, tools, and other resources for the small business owner to build the foundation for success while saving time and money!

www.BackOfficeTips.com

Welcome to My "Snow Globe"

by Deana Petrelli

t's easy to look inside a snow globe's calm scene and assume everything is perfect. We never stop to think of all the disruptions that happened throughout its existence.

When I was younger, I was a beauty queen and model who participated in ribbon cuttings and product endorsements. There was a struggle inside me because I never felt "good enough." I mistakenly relied on "other people" to measure my worth instead of looking inside myself. These experiences left me feeling devalued and untrusting. I went through the trauma of the suicide of my boyfriend. He ended his life after we broke up. I spent the next few years in a dysfunctional relationship with another man before I had the courage to walk away.

I finally embraced "my worth" and pursued a male-dominated career. I wanted people to appreciate my talent, drive, and determination. I also wanted other people to see that "success" is only limited by your own thoughts.

When I met my husband, I told him that I would "never" get married, have children, or be a stay-at-home mom. He was special. I married him and broke all my rules.

Eighteen years later, life was comfortably humming along. We had a great life, but like a lot of people, we were struck with unexpected circumstances that devastated us financially. Unfortunately, we invested our money and trust incorrectly.

In the blink of an eye everything had changed. Our security was snatched from under us. We had never had this type of financial despair before. I thought we had planned for everything, but in life you can't. This situation was completely out of our control. If you've been to this place, you know my pain.

I cried a lot about the possibility of losing everything we had ever worked for. Then I got on my knees and surrendered, asking, "show me what I need to do here for my family."

I suddenly remembered reading a James Malinchak book that said, "In every situation, you can only have two things: excuses or solutions." This was my tipping point. I picked myself up, dusted myself off, and intentionally decided that this nightmare and I were going to battle.

I sat down and wrote a list of all my life experience and skills. It's so funny how we can have naturally be doing something well for years and not even realize it. Especially when the rest of the world seems to clearly see what you're meant to be doing!

Staring at my list, it dawned on me that over the years hundreds of people had come and were still coming to me because they trusted my honest opinion on products, services, or entertainment. I was their one-stop-resource on what was hot, not, or what was trending, etc.

People say that I am unusually perceptive, skilled, and creative. It doesn't seem to matter if it is fashion, makeup, or custom car design. My skills seem to cross all borders, yielding great results.

I naturally seek out, try, or test things I find an interest in. I hate wasting time or money, so I tend to be more diligent than most before determining my opinion on anything. I am inspired to use products in new or unusual ways to express myself, and I like trying new things. Over the years, I have developed a hardcore knack for finding savvy products that perform well at sensible prices. People are drawn to this and find value in my opinions. It didn't dawn on me even once over the years that this could be a career option.

I spent the next few months going to every business seminar I could find, including Craig Duswalt's RockStar System for Success Bootcamp. I read, researched, learned, absorbed, and applied every nugget of knowledge I could. I decided I was "all in" with my last penny and last drop of courage.

Only in this desperate place would I take the risks necessary to push my boundaries. I found potential in myself that I didn't even know I had! In three months, I had created my official brand, "Petrelli Reviews," a lifestyle radio show, website, blog, and YouTube channel, where people join me on my plus-size adventures as I review products, services, and entertainment.

I'd never been a fan of social media, but I embraced it. I went from being invisible online to being a radio show host and YouTube personality, which was completely out of my comfort zone. I decided to get back into modeling, but this time as a plus-size woman. I entered another beauty pageant, as I wanted to be an example for people who feel like they aren't good enough, because in actuality they are more than good enough!

Within two months of using social media, and not having even launched my website, my company gained 2,000 followers. It's been less than six months now, and I have been filmed for a popular TV show, co-authored two published books, written for a magazine, and have interviewed numerous celebrities on the red carpet, representing my company. I fought and won. I have achieved things I never dreamed were possible.

Looking back now, I see that life is a lot like a snow globe. For those of you who are struggling, looking from the outside in, remember that the history of a snow globe isn't always visible or perfect. In fact, I've found sometimes it needs to be frantically shaken up, pouring down bad weather before things settle. Ultimately, everything falls back into perfect harmony.

Deana Petrelli is a radio show host, YouTuber, author, speaker, reviewer, and lifestyle blogger. Deana created "Petrelli Reviews," a marketing and publicity company specializing in helping businesses improve brand recognition and online presence through sharing her honest review findings on multiple media and technology platforms.

www.PetrelliReviews.com

EVERYTHING I TOUCH
TURNS TO SUCCESS

by Suzy Prudden

M y first success occurred with the fact that I was born, alive. Eight years previously, my mother, on her first day of skiing, fell and broke her pelvis in five places. She was told she'd never walk again and, of course, never have children. She went on to become the nation's foremost fitness authority, started The President's Council on Physical Fitness and Sports, and had two children, both girls.

Needless to say, I was born cesarean, and if she hadn't broken her pelvis and had her children without surgery, I would have been born dead, as the umbilical cord was wrapped around my throat, and I would have strangled to death on the way out of her womb.

Everything I touch turns to success, even failure. Who else would flunk seventh grade with straight F's? After years of success as a fitness expert, television personality, author (eleven books with New York's finest publishers and the New York Times Best Seller list before the Internet), body/mind pioneer, and empowerment coach as early as 1987, I lost everything and ended up homeless eight months after being the hour long subject on Oprah with my book "Metfitness®: Your Thoughts Taking Shape" (Hay House).

As a celebrity and household name, it was totally shaming. I lost all self-respect. How could I have done that to myself? Nobody did it to me; I did it all to myself. It was a long and terrifying journey back but freeing and exciting at the same time. It was a major opportunity for learning and growth, which is an entire story unto itself.

I think my most favorite question I was ever asked was asked at a party in 1997. It was a Rave. I had gone with my cousin, Katrina, an artist and college professor living on a houseboat in Sausalito on the Bay.

The Rave was held on a boat that circled San Francisco Bay for four or five hours. There were three decks with three different DJ's, three different styles of music, and a light show on the mountains next to San Francisco Bay.

I was talking to a friend of my cousin who was asking questions about my life. As I told her, she suddenly stopped me and said, "Are you a pathological liar?" I laughed and said, "No, why?" She said, "Nobody has a life like that."

"I do," I replied. And I do.

When I was asked to write a success story, I have to say, my whole life is a success story.

Has it been easy? Sometimes.

Has it been hard? Sometimes.

Have I been smart? Sometimes.

Have I been stupid? Sometimes.

Have I made smart moves? Yes.

Have I made mistakes? Definitely.

Have I accomplished a lot? Yes.

Do I sometimes trigger people? Yes.

Do others think I'm wonderful? Sure.

Have I been living life fully? All the time.

Do I like myself? Absolutely.

I actually think I'm my best company, and since I live with myself 24/7, I think that's my biggest success of all.

But wait, there's more!

I have a fifty-year-long career of being out front. My name has been on every business I have owned, and every TV show I have starred in, and every book I have ever written. "Suzy Prudden's" this and "Suzy Prudden's" that. I'm the product. And that's exhausting.

I have a very strong relationship with God. Some people call it The Universe, some people call it Jesus, some people call it The Force. I call that which is greater than all things God.

I am not religious, but I do believe. I am a spiritual being having a human experience. And I also believe in miracles. I ask for them all the time, and I receive them all the time. There's a whole book I could write about the miracles I have received.

Last year was a rough year for me. I was truly tired and bored with my business, and I'm not in a position, even at age 72 with all of my successes, of stopping. I started to ask God to bring me something more exciting, something bigger than me, something bigger than "Suzy Prudden."

During the Christmas holidays this past year, my sister came to visit for two days. While she was here, we reworked a book we had published in 2006 that wasn't doing anything. She redid the cover, cut a lot of the information out, simplified it, and took my name off the cover!

My name has been on everything I've done for the past fifty years! After my ego did a mini upset, I looked at the cover and said, "Petie, we have a brand here. This is a multi-million dollar company and one we can actually sell in three to five years if we want to." The title went from "Suzy Prudden's Itty Bitty…" to "Your Amazing Itty Bitty Weight Loss Book." That simple shift, taking my name off the cover, freed me and gave us a company.

I call us the new "Dummies." The difference is, when you read a 350-page "Dummies" book, you have to read it with a yellow highlighter. We are the yellow highlights! We are only fifteen steps. Every book covers a certain niche. Every book is only thirty-five pages long.

They look alike, they have the same format, and they are known for giving concise, accurate information on the niche they are covering.

My sister, the writer, and I, the in front of the camera person, get to do everything we've done for ourselves in the past to benefit our authors going forward. We each get to take our expertise and 100 years of combined experience and shepherd our authors to their successes.

With the stroke of a pen we created a multi-million dollar business, our retirement, and an opportunity for a lot of wonderful people to get their message out there and make a name for themselves. They're going to make a lot of money and create opportunities at the same time.

––––––––––

Suzy Prudden is an internationally acclaimed speaker, author, and seminar leader and the President and Co-Founder of Itty Bitty Publishing, where she publishes short books for niche markets. Suzy speaks to entrepreneurs and business owners on how to achieve success in their niche and use their expertise to position themselves in the forefront of their field.

www.ittybittypublishing.com

PhD RockStar in Progress

by Denise Schickel

B
ecause it's there" was the famous response by George H. Mallory in 1924 when asked why he wanted to climb Mt. Everest, the highest peak in the world. The very existence of Mt. Everest has remained a challenge to the climbing community up to the present day.

For me, having a PhD was the highest peak. I dreamed of having a PhD when I was an undergraduate. But I wasn't earning much money and graduate school was expensive.

Meanwhile, I have always been athletic, so I got a job as a massage therapist and enjoyed the work for many years. It was physically demanding, and kept me healthy, but I always felt something was missing. To satisfy my intellectual curiosity, I read books in my spare time.

Realizing I wanted a relationship, I finally met the man of my dreams; he projected a bright and beautiful future for us together.

I finally had everything I ever wanted—a satisfying job, a beautiful relationship, a future I had only dreamed about, and I was still young enough to enjoy it.

Then one day, after two years, he disappeared. No goodbye, no break up, no message.

I was completely devastated. Not only did I lose my great romance, but, most of all; I lost the future we had planned together.

I felt I had nothing; I felt like a loser. All of a sudden I was more alone that I had been before. I had been presented with great happiness, and then it had been taken away.

I didn't know how to escape from the despair that enveloped me. Now my work, which had previously been satisfying, was no longer enough. I searched inside myself to find a way out of the pain I was feeling. How could I create meaning and a future for myself?

After much soul searching, I realized what I needed to do. I had to go to graduate school, immediately. I knew that would lead me back to meaning and happiness.

I asked my friends, do you think I can do this? Am I too old? But what else could I do, older than the other students or not, I knew it was the only way out. I decided to just do it.

There was nothing I could do about being over 50, but there was a lot I could do about creating a new future for myself.

I started researching graduate schools. I wanted to study psychology, but which specialty? I heard about an evolving field, Industrial/Organizational psychology. A light bulb went off in my mind; I knew this was just what I wanted even though I was not really sure what it was!

Oh yes, I was scared; I hadn't been in academia in decades. How hard would it be? How smart am I? How smart are the other students? Is it too late?

Later that same year I entered a master's program. The first semester I had a headache for a month. I read my assignments two or three times until they sank in. It was all so new, and I loved being in class again.

When the verdict of the first semester grades was handed down, I had three A's for three courses. It was the first time in my life I had gotten all A's. I was so happy.

I felt validated and uplifted with the possibility of a satisfying future ahead of me.

I was so inspired by my grades that I became determined to keep it up— and I did. Throughout my entire M.A. program I got all A's, graduating with summa cum laude inscribed on my diploma. This experience so motivated me that I continued on for the PhD that I had dreamed about.

I found an online program and, after a three-month break, got into a PhD program. For the last several years I have taken one course a quarter, with a couple of three-month breaks. I have continued to get A's in all my courses.

This accomplishment gives me a tremendous sense of fulfillment. I am so excited about my future in a new career. Now I finally feel complete. This continuing education has developed me in new ways and given me a deeper level of satisfaction and meaning than I had before. I am so happy that I was driven to go to graduate school.

My graduate education, along with my 30 years' experience as a massage therapist, has blended into what is becoming the development of self-care strategies for individuals. I am working on books for self-care for massage therapists, and better aging, which will be published in 2016.

Looking back, I see how many obstacles emerged in my path, forcing me to change direction. I remembered Bruce Lee's words: "Be like water," and I have allowed myself to flow around the obstacles. It has required a mixture of courage and optimism—a faith that everything will work out.

Making a career change at a stage in life when most people are preparing for retirement is unusual. It is difficult to make changes anytime, but when you know it is the inevitable next phase of your evolution, it is easy. I feel like I'm swimming with the current. Sometimes it is very strong and scary, but it is my journey.

What guided me through these changes are three basic ideas.

First, know thyself. What makes you happy? What are your talents and interests? What motivates you?

Second, what kind of life fits your character and how you want to live? How can you create a life that allows you to be authentic?

Third, experiment and continue to learn throughout your life. You may go through some major changes as different parts of your personality emerge. Don't be afraid to try new activities.

When life gets difficult, remember the Japanese proverb: Fall down eight times, get up nine.

Denise Schickel is a massage therapist who is evolving into an author, speaker, and industrial psychologist who provides self-care strategies for individuals in diverse environments.

www.SelfCareExpert.com

Turning a Penchant for Secrets into a Career

By Judy Schriener

E ver since I was a little kid, people have been telling me their secrets. I'm not sure how it started. The first time it made an impression on me that maybe I had a special gift for getting people to tell me their innermost thoughts and secrets was in high school. A neighbor girl in one of my high school classes invited me over to her house one day and told me about some of her adventures. I listened attentively, didn't interrupt her, asked her a few "how" and "why" questions, and I nodded a lot. Afterward, she looked at me with a puzzled expression and said, "You're not shocked, and you're not judging me." In the decades since, I've heard that over and over. That and, "I've never told anyone this before."

From early, early childhood, I've been a curious person. Yes, I want to know how things work. But mostly I want to know how people think and feel. I live to know how people think and feel. I live to learn who people are behind their public façade and why they do things.

After college, I went into advertising as a career. I worked for two ad agencies, I wrote ad copy for clients of a radio station, I sold radio time, I sold graphic arts services, I ran an in-house advertising agency for a large car dealer, I managed advertising for a large real estate company with seventeen offices, and I was the Director of Advertising for the Arizona Lottery, the first lottery west of the Mississippi, when it launched.

In each of those stints, I got close to the people I dealt with, whether they were colleagues, clients, or vendors. They told me amazing things about themselves, from the moment one knew his marriage was over, to how a woman pulled off cheating on her husband without his knowledge, and then one man showed me pictures of himself indulging his obsession with cross-dressing. (The secrets weren't all about sex but, after all, that's where a lot of secrets lie.)

Then a divorce—mine—nearly brought me down, both personally and career-wise. I needed a change.

I saw an ad for a writer/reporter for a small weekly business newspaper in Phoenix, Arizona, where I lived. I'd never written for a publication, but I knew I was a good writer, a fast learner, a thorough and detailed researcher, and I knew I could get people to talk to me. I got the gig.

The way I learned to write for publication was that I turned in my stories and when they ran, I went over them line by line to see what my editors had changed. Soon they weren't changing very much at all.

Best of all, I got people to talk to me. I was truly interested in them as people. I could easily read people when we were face to face, but I was scared to do interviews over the phone, which I had to start doing when I interviewed people outside Arizona. Amazingly, I could hear so many clues over the phone—how they breathed, when they hesitated, what they emphasized—that soon I could "read" them at least as well over the phone.

That little writing gig led to a thirty-year career in journalism, where I got paid—sometimes well paid!—to indulge my curiosity and get people to talk to me. I've lived and worked in New York City and Washington, D.C., I've written a professional book that McGraw-Hill published and sold for sixty dollars each, and I've traveled all over the world.

I chose business journalism because I wanted access to the best minds in business rather than "the public." Business people—executives and entrepreneurs—are among the smartest and most optimistic people in the world. And I've gotten to interview literally thousands of them over the years. Some were celebrities—they have ties to business, too—and nearly all were accomplished, successful people. Business people are generally very accessible to journalists. If they didn't want to talk, I would tell them, "We're going to do a story on you/your company either way, and we'd rather do it with your input." In some very unlikely cases, I got my interview by saying that, but mostly I got the interview by referring them to other people they respected who vouched for me.

Keeping people's secrets became a way of life. People told me things that could send them to prison if they got out. They ratted on each other and sneaked me confidential documents, and I had to keep to myself who they were. I told people, "I'll go to jail before I'll reveal that you're my source." I never had to go to jail, but I remember how excited I was when one company threatened to sue me if I used a document they didn't want to get out. "I'm doing something important, or they wouldn't want to sue me!" I thought. I used it. They didn't sue me.

Over the years, I've written countless stories and profiles of people who run companies. Mostly, people trusted me and told me the whole story. I urged them to tell me sensitive details "off the record" and then got many of them to permit me to use those same details "on the record." They trusted me to be fair.

I got awards and recognition. What was more important to me was getting access to the people I wanted to talk to and getting them to open up to me. I've gotten great info and insight from people I was told would never crack. And nearly all talked to me multiple times afterward.

I've never aspired to be on radio or television. "The delete key is my best friend," I'd tell people. But things change. I have hosted a radio show, "Off the Record with Judy," for upward of three years. Every show is themed "Secrets of…," and I've interviewed many successful people and a handful of celebrities. Mostly, I just get interesting, successful people to open up and share their secrets. I live for that, and I've gotten paid to do just that for the last thirty years. How lucky am I?!

———————

Judy Schriener is an award-winning journalist, author, and radio show host who has interviewed thousands of executives and entrepreneurs in her thirty-year career. After writing a business book published by McGraw-Hill—*Building for Boomers: Guide to Design and Construction*—she is now focusing on writing books about relationships.

www.offtherecordwithjudy.com

HOW DESPAIR INSPIRED MY LIFE'S WORK

by Susan Sheppard

I n 1983, I was lonely, sad, and confused. I had just turned 40, and it seemed like my life was in a shambles. We had lost our homes to foreclosure, both the investment property and our family home. The business partnership that I had considered to be solid was suddenly dramatically brought to an end, and we were about to be homeless, broke, and unemployed. What went wrong?

My despair was noticeable. We were both intelligent, educated, and capable, and yet we were staring into the face of marital, financial and emotional disaster. We loved each other, but that wasn't enough. We weren't getting what we wanted at all. We needed help.

I sought counseling for Viet Nam veterans' families. Bob, my husband of 17 years, had been a Green Beret who served for two years in Viet Nam. I really didn't know about his tour, because the subject had been completely off limits.

During 25 PTSD (Post Traumatic Stress Disorder) screening questions, I agreed that he didn't beat me and he wasn't a drug abuser. The other questions about nightmares and sleeping with a gun under his pillow and inability to stay employed and contempt for authority struck me in the heart, and I realized we were living in a world outside the realm of normal. The nurse paused, then suggested that I must be a strong woman. I was crying. I had been doing crisis intervention as an RN in Emergency Services since age 20, and I could not save us.

Our family went to the Viet Nam Vet Center a few times, but Bob was unwilling to talk about the war and refused to return. The girls, ages 15, 12, and 5, were rebelling against any kind of counseling. I was very frustrated, and I still didn't completely understand his issues. Finally, I gave him an ultimatum that he either use his three degrees to get a teaching job or get out.

Bob taught for three years, but when he ignored the district rules, the administration dismissed him. Then after a three-year construction project, both he and the Marine veteran who owned the construction company were waiting for work to appear.

I started to tell Bob I was leaving him, and he interrupted the conversation to make a phone call. I took that personally.

I didn't realize it was his way of coping. My heart was broken, and I did what I usually did when things didn't work out, which was to take every course I could find to learn. This time it was about relationships. I wanted to know how to love, be classy, and still get what I wanted.

I loved Bob but I couldn't fix this situation. I just didn't know what to do. My two oldest daughters were living on their own. Bob and our youngest stayed in the house, and I went to live alone. The day I left I spent 24 hours vomiting and crying. I filed for divorce. Bob never acknowledged our divorce, and it finalized two years later without his signature.

So far this story sounds like failure, not success, but there is more to the story.

After the divorce, I met and was dating a charming man who was 18 years younger, foreign born, and the eldest of seven children. To make matters worse, his mother and I were the same age. Our romantic relationship didn't survive, but we remained very close friends. He resumed dating his younger girlfriend. I was able to observe their very dramatic two-year courtship as his friend and her "enemy rival for his attention."

Toward the end of that two years, she asked to talk to me. I responded, "Why? You don't even like me." Admitting to that, she said, "I have decided that he is not what I want. I have been watching while I have been his girlfriend and you have been his friend, and he is different with you than he is with me.

It is like I have had his body and you have had his soul, and I want to know how to do that with a man. Will you teach me?"

I was shocked and said no. She persisted for several months until I agreed to a short-term coaching trial. Ultimately, this young woman became my first relationship client. We spoke daily for the next two years. During that time, I shared my story and everything I had learned to help her get what she wanted. I realized it was more fun to talk about love and sex than crisis intervention.

I developed my Love with CLASS system, which is even more perfected today. In the past 25 years, I have successfully coached hundreds of singles to get what they want in the way of a relationship. The young woman, now a dear friend, is still successfully married to someone she had known, but couldn't "see," before we expanded her perception of men.

As for me, I learned to turn my personal disaster into my life's work. I learned that I am a healer and an influencer and that my experience and knowledge offers hope to people with broken or wounded hearts. I learned that I make a difference and that my clients "trust me more than they are afraid" to own their personal power, expand their comfort zone, and grow.

Although I didn't save my own marriage, Bob and I remained very close friends and parents to our three beautiful daughters until his sudden death in 1999. If I had known in that first seventeen years of marriage what I know now about relationships, things might have been different for us.

My company is called Getting What You Want. As a life coach specializing in relationships, I use my Love with CLASS system to heal wounded hearts, grow self-esteem, and teach personal power and to ask for what you want in a way that you will be heard. I'm still saving lives, but now I save hearts as well.

––––––––––

Susan Sheppard is a professional speaker, author, coach, and creator of Getting What You Want, Inc. Susan speaks to singles who want a relationship about men–women differences, raising self-esteem, and getting what you want in life. Susan is healing one relationship at a time with her unique Love with CLASS system.

www.gettingwhatyouwant.com

A LIFE RE-ENGINEERED

by Alan Skidmore

W hat do you want to be when you grow up?

This is a question asked of young folks throughout the generations.

And me? Well, I had originally wanted to be a doctor. That was my plan until I entered college; however, after spending a year as a Biology major, I realized that maybe I was on the wrong track.

It has been said that whatever you are interested in during your early teens is most likely your true calling. My interests had been music, electronics, and gadgets, so I decided that maybe I should become an Electrical Engineer. After a multitude of technical classes and a ridiculous amount of math, I earned my coveted EE degree.

For the next thirty years I had a successful career as an Electrical Engineer, working in the automotive manufacturing, chemical, natural gas, and cable TV industries.

Not long after graduation, I married Penny, and within a few years we had two sons, Justin and Jesse. While my mom and dad had instilled a good work ethic in me, I eventually discovered that work becomes less about passion and more about a need to provide for a growing family. That's not a bad thing, but no one ever tells us this early in our lives. I suppose if we were told the truth, most of us would stay home and live with our parents forever.

Around the time I was 30, I began listening to a lot of personal development programs and started attending seminars to learn what is not taught in the normal school curriculum.

A major shift in my life came around the time I turned 50. I wasn't afraid of turning fifty, nor was it all that big of a deal; yet, when I stopped to think about it, I would wonder, "Where did the years go, how did I get this old already, and what I have been doing?"

During my fiftieth birthday party, which included black balloons, a stuffed crow, and birthday cards jokingly telling me that I was "over the hill," I had an epiphany. I told everyone that I was not over the hill, but that my fiftieth birthday was "the first day of the second half of my life!"

I decided then and there that I was going to have more fun in my life, which started almost immediately, though my life up until that time had certainly not been dull!

During my forties, I had become involved with Toastmasters International to learn how to be a better public speaker. From this training and because I wanted to share my knowledge, I began to speak at different events. In 2010, I was asked to speak at a technology conference in Melbourne, Australia, and again in Las Vegas. During that summer, just for fun, my youngest son and I went to Ghana, Africa, with a group from our church to help improve an orphanage that we supported. That was a life-changing experience, and I learned that the whole world was not like the United States.

My son and I also learned that kids can be happy with just the basics, and that all we really need is a roof over our head, clothing, food, and to share our love with others. And one of the best ways to improve your life is to discover the gifts that you have been given and then use those gifts to make the world a better place.

Just a few months before my fiftieth birthday, I was laid off from work for the third time in less than ten years. At this point, I was fed up with the corporate world and decided to work for myself and opened shop as an IT consultant. Also around this time, I attended my first RockStar Marketing Bootcamp with Craig Duswalt, where I met Glenn Morshower (Aaron Pierce of "24" and numerous other Hollywood movies and TV shows), who has become a dear, close friend and a "brother from another mother."

By joining a group of like-minded people who wanted to make the world a better place, I discovered some of my gifts.

For me, that happened by becoming involved in the RockStar MasterMind program and taking many of the ideas learned from some great minds and applying them to my own life and business. Since then, I have grown my IT consulting business where I have more work coming to me than I can handle. As a result of one of these IT projects, I was offered and accepted a position as the IT Director for West Virginia State University. I certainly didn't see that one coming!

Then, really stepping out of the "norm," in 2013, I launched an Internet radio show called "Prime Time Success Radio with Alan Skidmore." This adventure allowed me to share wisdom with folks from all over the world and to interview some very well-known experts, including Bob Burg, Dan Miller, and "The Pitbull of Personal Development," Larry Winget.

Over the past five years, I have traveled nearly around the world, met numerous rock stars and celebrities, and made friends with some of the most amazing people on earth. How did I do this? I changed my attitude, I decided that I was going to have more fun, and I stepped up and said "yes!" to all those opportunities that have appeared right in front of me.

I am often asked, "How does a country boy from West Virginia get to meet all these wonderful folks and do such cool things?" I tell them to step out, get on a plane, or jump in the car…and go!

You can get to just about anywhere on earth within 24 hours. So do something out of the ordinary. Turn off the TV, get off your smartphone, and stop watching other folks live their dreams. Go live your own! Move out of your comfort zone, get uncomfortable, and take a chance. Decide that you are here for a reason, discover that reason, and then pursue that mission with great passion!

―――――――――

Alan has worked as an Electrical Engineer and is now is an IT consultant where he speaks around the country and internationally. He is the author of "The Common Sense Guide to Life" and the host of "Prime Time Success Radio." He lives in West Virginia with his wife and two sons.

www.alanskidmore.com

A Mom's Story of Success

by Barbara Starley

Success is an interesting word. Ask ten people for their definition of success, and you are likely to get ten different answers. My "RockStar" moment came as a result of a punishment imposed on my son, which triggered a series of "RockStar" opportunities for him as well.

It started out with a typical parent–teacher conference at the end of the first semester of my son's eighth grade year, his last year of Junior High at Edu-Prize Charter School. I loved visiting the classrooms, meeting Colton's teachers, and seeing all the projects on display. The halls were lined with posters, and the classrooms were filled with incredible hands-on learning projects that the students had created throughout the semester. It was obvious that the kids worked hard and were engaged in what they were learning.

As we left that day, I was one proud mom! Colton's teachers loved having him in their classes and sang his praises as a model student, particularly when it came to anything that involved art. We talked about all that he was learning and how delighted we were that we had decided to stay at that school for junior high.

Then I asked him about a writing assignment that I saw on display in his history classroom and that I hadn't been able to find his. Colton explained that the assignment had been an "honors" project, and because he already had an "A" in the class, he had chosen not to do it. There was only one problem... we had an agreement that he would do all honors projects. He insisted that he saw absolutely no reason to do the honors project because he had a 104 percent in the class already, without doing it. Except for one thing…we had an agreement that he would do all honors projects.

The whole purpose for honors projects, in Colton's mind, was to get extra credit in the class and potentially raise his grade. But in my mind, the honors projects were more about challenging the students and giving them a chance to go above and beyond what the average student would do. Besides…we had an agreement that he would do all honors projects.

With that being said, I simply and (surprisingly) calmly told him that I expected him to complete the history project anyway—over Christmas break—and the real bummer was that he would get no school credit for the work he did. "I can't believe you're going to make me do that stupid project for no good reason," he said. But I had a good reason, we had an agreement, and I expected him to honor it. The rest of the ride home was very quiet.

After some time of sulking in his room, Colton came to me with a proposition.

"That assignment that you're going to make me do was a writing assignment," he stated. "And it was for history class, right?" I agreed. "Well, if I write about history, can I write about anything I want?"

I was curious. "What did you have in mind?" I inquired.

"Well, I have an idea for a book. I already wrote the first chapter."

I looked up from the work I was doing. "What is it about?" I asked.

"The story takes place during World War I, which is what we are studying in History class."

"Okay," I said, "but you have to write every day during Christmas break, deal?"

And just like that, we had a deal. Colton got to write about what he wanted to write about, and I still felt that he was honoring our agreement.

We spent most of the next three weeks at our cabin in the mountains, away from all the distractions at home. Every day, without being told, Colton would disappear into his room and type a chapter of his book. I loved it when he bounded down the stairs to tell me that his book was really taking shape, or that I was going to really like the chapter he had just written.

I could see the excitement on his face as Colton revealed only bits and pieces of the story each day. One day he came down and told me that I was not going to like the way one particular chapter ended; one of his characters had been killed. "This book takes place during World War I," he reminded me.

After three weeks, Colton had written twenty-one chapters. He put the final touches on his book over the next several weeks. We found a self-publishing company that would print-on-demand, and over the next year, I watched that book bless others, open doors, and give him opportunities that few kids enjoy.

Colton was invited to the retirement party of his third grade teacher. As we walked in, Mrs. Curtis greeted us and asked how his drawing was coming along, and then inquired, "…and what about writing? Are you writing, Colton? I always pegged you as a writer." Little did she know that in just a few moments, Colton would read a tribute to Mrs. Curtis and present her with a copy of his first book—dedicated to her!

When the World War I traveling museum came to Mesa, Arizona, Colton was invited to set up a table and sell his books to the hundreds of mostly elderly people waiting in line. It was heartwarming to watch him interact with many people who had stories of their own, of relatives and friends they knew that fought in the war.

Colton's book received a Silver Medal by Moonbeam Children's Book Awards for "Best Book by a Young Author," and a local newspaper wrote a story about him and an 88-year-old author entitled "Never Too Young—or Old—to Write a Book."

But my real "RockStar" moment came when Colton was invited to speak on stage at the Author 101 conference in Las Vegas. He had an audience of over 600 adults laughing, cheering, and applauding as he retold the story of our "agreement" and how the "relentless coaxing of his mother" was the beginning of his book, *Aura*.

Barbara Starley is a Christian, CPA, Certified QuickBooks® Pro Advisor, Certified LivePlan® Expert Advisor, speaker, author, wife, and mom. Barbara does QuickBooks® set-up, training, and troubleshooting for entrepreneurs and small business owners and serves as their On-Call Controller™ on an as-needed basis.

www.BarbaraStarley.com

RISK AND REWARD

by Karen Strauss

To quit or not to quit! That is the question.

I had worked hard in the publishing industry. As a publicist and then later sales manager, I had worked with many celebrities and New York Times best-selling authors.

In the early 90s, I had a great job working as a sales director at a major publishing company.

I was on the verge of buying a co-op apartment in New York City.

I was 34 and had a great social life.

All good reasons for staying put! On the other hand, I was yearning to go out on my own, break free of corporate walls, and finally start my own business.

Oh! Yes—I only had about $3,000 in the bank. I didn't say I earned a lot of money in this glamorous industry.

I knew that over 50 percent of all small businesses fail within the first five years. Forbes said recently that 80 percent of entrepreneurs failed in 18 months. But for me, failure was not an option. I was young, hungry, and passionate and had a very expensive apartment to pay for.

I remember going out to my beach house on Fire Island that summer (my favorite place on Earth) and, over many glasses of champagne, discussing the pros and cons with my friends. They were incredibly supportive and kept cheering me on to do it. (Maybe because we were drunk!)

So I took the plunge—I quit my job and set up shop in my very expensive new apartment. So much for new furniture!

My first client was a Christian publisher called Fleming Revell. They were looking to expand their audience from Christians shopping in Christian bookstores to a more general constituency. My job was to sell their books into large retail stores like Barnes & Noble, Borders, Walden, Costco, and Sam's Club.

As it happened, they owned a small publishing house called Wynwood Press—The Editor-in-Chief had discovered an unknown author named John Grisham and immediately bought "Time to Kill." They published the book in hardcover and sold about 5,000 copies. By the time I was on board, John Grisham had published "The Firm" and had become a New York Times bestselling author. I was able to take "Time to Kill" into the top retailers and wholesalers and sell about 50,000 copies in a record amount of time. And Fleming Revell had their first New York Times bestselling book.

I thought wow! Owning a new business is easy. My first book was a John Grisham novel that I got to sell to my best friend—the fiction buyer at Barnes & Noble—and the other buyers that I had gotten to know well from my other corporate jobs running sales departments at major publishing houses.

I was a hero… a genius. A rock star! This Christian publishing company was very impressed with the "nice Jewish girl" they hired from New York City.

This is what I had signed up for. After paying my dues for so long working for someone else—I now had the opportunity to take things into my own hands.

Not so fast! Although this was an amazing start to my new career—it certainly didn't follow that smooth trajectory. Over the years, I have had many ups and downs. I have lost clients that represented over half my revenue. There were many times I just wanted to give up and look for a "steady" job. But I persevered. I changed my mindset. I decided that I would not give up. Instead of feeling sorry for myself, I would be intentional about finding new clients. I knew I was a really good "networker." I always enjoyed meeting people and figuring out how we could work together. What amazed me was how many of my Christian clients would recommend me to other publishers. That was when it really dawned on me that "reputation" was everything. My name was all I had—finally—my famous bluntness and honesty was being rewarded!

I learned that "cash is king"—there were going to be months when I made a lot of money and then other months when I could barely pay my bills. I needed to roll with the punches and make sure I had enough of a reserve to cover those lean times.

The scariest time came in 2011 when Borders closed. Borders was my biggest account, and I worked on commission. In addition, eBooks were on the rise, and I was not paid for eBooks sold by Barnes & Noble or Borders. This was definitely eating into my profits.

I was at a crossroads. The industry was forever changing. The landscape was quite different—Borders had closed, Barnes & Noble was shrinking, and Amazon was gaining market share. It was then I learned that an entrepreneur always needed to be flexible and forever changing. I could not stand still with my business when everything else around me was moving.

I decided to change up my business and concentrate on working with self-published authors to help market their books and get wider distribution.

It was around this time that I met Craig Duswalt. He was speaking in New York City about how to market like a "RockStar," and he inspired me to get out of my comfort zone and travel to Los Angeles to attend his RockStar Bootcamp.

Although I did not know any one of the 500 people in the room—I was comfortable with his topic. Marketing yourself and your business to stand out in a crowd begins with publishing a book! Aha! Now we are talking!

I joined his MasterMind Program, and it was there that the next idea for a business popped into my head. Create branded publishing companies for organizations. And so, Duswalt Press was born.

Starting my own company was the scariest thing I have ever done. I risked everything, but it was the greatest thing I have ever done. I still get chills when a campaign is successful. I enjoy working with publishers and authors. I feel rewarded when my clients are happy.

I now understand that while it's not an easy road—for me it was the most exhilarating and satisfying path I could have taken.

———————

Karen Strauss has held management and marketing positions at major publishing houses such as Crown, Random House, and Avon. Strauss Consultants works with authors and other organizations to maximize sales and marketing potential. She is the author of *Book Publishing for Entrepreneurs: Top Secrets from a New York Publisher.*

www.StraussConsultants.com

FROM CODEPENDENCY TO "INDEPENDENCY"

by Scott Transue

G rowing up in a highly-dysfunctional, addicted household can be brutal. You learn the three rules for survival very quickly: Don't talk, don't trust, and don't feel. Those rules work well while you're a child and not yet responsible for your own life. They are outright dangerous rules to live by as an adult.

I kept living those rules into early adulthood, and paid the price. One abusive relationship after another, getting stuck in "dead end" jobs, and not getting promoted into higher-skilled positions. It all culminated when a total nervous breakdown struck, the result of stress from the unrealistic demands of a dysfunctional workplace. I wound up in the hospital for a week. Quite frankly, I had lost the will to live. I did not care anymore.

I was released from the hospital and started on a path of intense therapy.

Deep inside, I knew I was on earth to do something special. After all, there must have been a reason for all the pain I had experienced. As destiny would have it (I no longer believe in "luck"), I located a company on the Internet that advocated for adults dealing with trauma. I inquired, and spent three years with them as a work-from-home advocate.

With a newly-found sense of self-esteem, I was browsing LinkedIn once day and noticed a profile for a recruiter for a national seminar company.

Mind you, I had been speaking for free with Toastmasters for years. The recruiter and I connected, and I asked whether they were looking for speakers. It was a question I would not have asked years before, thinking I was not good enough.

The recruiter said "Absolutely. Put together a video of you speaking to a group, and I will run it past our screening committee." I was simultaneously thrilled and scared to death. I had my Toastmasters club create the video for me and sent it in. About four days later, an email from the recruiter appeared. It read "Scott, call me. I need to discuss your video." I knew it… not good enough.

I called the recruiter and was asked when I might be available for an orientation call. "Orientation?" I asked. She said, "Well, yes. I thought you were interested in a speaking contract. Your video was one of the best we have seen this year." I almost dropped my cell phone. We scheduled a 90-minute orientation call and finalized plans for me to fly to Kansas for meetings with key staff.

Fast forward one year. I have now given seminars in over 25 states and have gotten contracts with three separate webinar companies. I have co-authored one book and have been a contributing author to another. Simply put, I feel like a RockStar, and it will only get better from here. I also now own two companies, a public speaking firm and a tax consulting firm.

I remember back to those extremely lonely days as a child and to that hospital stay that would change my life. I realize that God sometimes puts us into very negative circumstances so that we'll have something to share with the world as a result. After all, diamonds are created out of intense pressure.

So, if you need a speaker who can talk all about "making lemonade from lemons," I can help. If you need a very skilled tax professional, I can help. If you need someone to represent you or a loved one during the Social Security Disability process, I can help. If you know anyone who needs help in any of the above areas, contact me.

Even if you don't, however, remember the following. You're already great just as you are. No matter where you have come from, or what you have been through, you have something valuable to share with the world. Something no one else can share quite like you can. I found out what my message is. The only question is, what is yours? Once you figure that out, you will open up a world that, right now, may not even be conceivable for you. And maybe, just maybe, we can both share a stage and impact people around the world. So, when can we schedule your orientation call?

Scott Transue is a professional speaker, author, and tax professional. He presents seminars across the country on tax planning for small businesses and owns Freedom Day Tax and Accounting LLC.

www.ScottTransue.com

It's Never Too Late to Find Success, Happiness, or Your Soulmate

by Cynthia Trevino

Today I have much to be grateful for, a long-term marriage to my best friend, excellent health, and a successful consulting firm helping business owners grow their companies. I work with brave, bold entrepreneurs who are changing the world. They're creating innovative teaching videos for special needs kids, advancing water rights, and guiding technology startups. They inspire me every day.

But it wasn't always like this. Once I was a single, career-obsessed, corporate cubicle-dweller. Lean in? I leaned in so far in I fell flat on my face!

I traveled constantly as an AT&T staffer based in New Jersey. For one key project, I spent weeks on end in Nashville. I didn't realize how much time until one day at breakfast, the nice server came to my table and said my mom was on the phone. (Cell phones didn't exist yet.)

This was a wakeup call; the only way my mom could reach me was through the hotel staff! I missed this indicator that perhaps there was another way to live.

Next, an unmistakable indicator arrived. Headquarters cancelled the project, and along with it, my interim promotion. I was devastated. I'd been inching up the corporate ladder. I felt like a failure.

The director gave me time to locate my next internal assignment. As I took a deep breath and thought about who to call first, it struck me that I was at a crossroads. I had a moment of clarity. Instead of searching immediately for another position, I thought deeply. Where was my life going? What did I truly want? And for the first time, how do I want to feel?

My epiphany: Career success wasn't everything. My first passion was no longer about achieving corporate milestones or snagging bigger projects.

I discovered that I wanted to feel loved. To share my life with a man who cared about me, about how my day was. Someone who'd go shopping with me. Someone who'd enjoy sitting by the fire on snowy weekends, who'd suffer through occasional chick-flicks and who'd always have my back. I silently admitted that what I really wanted was a long-term relationship.

My moment of clarity resulted in an all-out search for a soulmate. Like any good project manager, I created a spreadsheet of local singles' events. This was before the Internet. Before match.com! The New York Times personal ads were my go-to resource.

Enduring the circus of bozos that frequented the 1989 singles scene wasn't exactly a picnic. When that became insane, without tangible results, I course-corrected and joined a singles' bicycling club. I met nicer men, got great exercise, and even lost weight!

The search for my soulmate was consuming, exhausting and, at times, discouraging.

My female friends called me delusional. "You think you're going to find a husband at your age? Really?" they sneered.

I kept my commitment to attend two singles events each week. It was a juggling act with long work hours. It often felt like a second job! But I persevered.

My best friend was mystified by my determination. "I don't know if you're the smartest woman I know or the stupidest," she remarked.

Two years into my search I realized that a coworker was the soulmate I was looking for. I discovered he was funny and smart, and we shared interests— bicycling, wine, foreign films, and favorite NYC art galleries. We got married the next year. That was 24 wonderful years ago.

Reflecting back to that time, I felt like a RockStar after finding the man of my dreams. My priorities had shifted. I stopped waking up each day fixated on career success. It was freeing. I saw the world through a fresh lens. I put my husband, my life and myself before my career.

I still did great work. I stepped up, just not as often. I secured projects requiring less travel.

I felt whole. Balanced (most of the time). I felt empathy for coworkers with family demands. Clearly, everyone had a personal life.

I'm forever grateful for that long-ago moment of clarity. For recognizing I was at a crossroads. For pausing a beat before diving into a job search. For the insight to get clarity about how I wanted to feel.

Remember my story when you find yourself at a crossroads, when your world shifts, when life dumps a truckload of lemons at your feet. Take three steps: 1) Get clear. 2) Get prepared. 3) Get going.

Step 1. Get clear. Clarify in your heart and mind not what to do next, but how you want to feel. Don't immediately choose your next move. Yours might be finding a soulmate, landing a massively well-paying job, exploring the world, starting a nonprofit, or building a business.

Before deciding on your next act, get crystal clear about how you want to feel. Do you want to feel—Fearless? Accomplished? Inspired? Fulfilled? Energized? Unstoppable? Settled? Maybe you want to feel all of these.

Choose three to five feelings that optimize your life. Use them to guide your decisions. Ask: Will choice a, b, or c help me feel (fill in the blank)?

Step 2. Get prepared. Don't pen a business or life plan yet. Make lists. Lists are easy and fun. Inventory things to answer, learn, solve, or discover before beginning your new chapter.

Are you going to relocate? Change industries? Go back to school? You're on a fact-finding mission! My lists were: Books about finding a husband, clothes for singles' events, and tips about great first date conversations.

Step 3. Get going. Get out of your comfort zone! As they say, what got you here isn't going to get you there! Decide what you're going to do differently to achieve your dreams or find the love of your life.

My husband made it possible for me to navigate the orchards of lemons dumped at my feet since 1992. I couldn't have done it without him.

I wish you clarity in choosing your next chapter.

Cynthia Trevino is an entrepreneur, blogger, speaker, marketing consultant, and co-founder of Resonnect, who focuses on business growth. Cynthia is on a mission to help 5,000 founders, owners, and entrepreneurs who are changing the world, one wonderful customer at a time.

www.cytrevino.com

THREE STRIKES YOU'RE OUT!
OR THIRD TIME'S THE CHARM?

by Nellie T Williams

Every overnight success takes time. Success is a result of trial and error. We correct and continue.

At age 24 I'd been in all my girlfriends' weddings and felt "always a bridesmaid, never a bride." I was attractive. I had a college degree. I wanted to be married, too.

When James said, "Let's get married," I said, "Okay." My mother said it was normal for a bride to be nervous on the evening before her wedding day. She was nervous the night before she married my dad, and they had been married then for 26 years. I didn't have the nerve to call off the wedding. I was afraid my marriage was over before the honeymoon was over. After 18 months, I found my courage and filed for divorce. Lesson learned: True, continual communication between spouses, between all people, is critical.

I don't remember Dan's proposal a few years later. Soon, for no reason on my part, Dan became jealous. His mistrust of me was just him projecting onto me his own bad behavior. When he got up his courage to tell me he'd had an affair, I wanted to explode. I'd always imagined any cheating husband of mine spread eagle on a rotating carnival-like wheel. Surely the daggers I would throw would hit their mark. I'd keep my eyes open for this one. Lesson learned: Pay attention to the signs along the way, no matter how painful.

My own calmness surprised me. I told him I never wanted this to happen again. I didn't want this one mistake to come between us. I wanted to put his affair behind us and never talk about it again. I loved him. Dan took my lack of wild-woman emotion as tacit endorsement for his continued bad behavior.

Almost ten years later, I divorced Dan for financial reasons. The property settlement was amicable. I laughingly tell my friends that I still use Dan's name because I bought it. I paid dearly for it. I had already established myself in business as Nellie Williams.

After several years of serial dating, I told God I wanted someone to share my life with. I told Him He'd done a wonderful job of filling my past lists of qualities I wanted in a partner, but my lists were faulty.

At age 50, I felt too old for the bar scene. I didn't know about computer dating services. When I told God that He knew the perfect man for me and that I'd be the perfect woman for him, I didn't realize I'd already met Steve. If Steve had told me the day we met that he'd called his mother that night and told her I've met 'The One'!" I would surely have run. I needed time.

Steve and I were neighbors. He knew I worked late during tax season. He invited me to knock on his door if I came home hungry and saw his lights on. He said he would have chicken-fried steak, mashed potatoes and gravy ready for me in fifteen minutes. I didn't believe him. Other people had spun me a lot of stories over the years. I've learned that Steve doesn't lie. We have never lied to each other.

Even today, the kitchen is his domain. He loves to watch my expression when he serves dinner and I take my first bite. Steve takes care of most of our meals. When it is my turn to cook, I make reservations. He doesn't even know I can cook.

I am so glad Steve found the courage one more time. He slid on his knees across his living room floor and put the biggest ring I'd ever seen on my left hand ring finger. He finally asked (for the first time) the big question, "Will you marry me?" He had suggested it three times but had never really asked until that fourth time. That biggest ring I'd ever seen was a nut off his '82 Ford truck. I still smile when I remember Steve's proposal.

Why had I waited? I was afraid. I already had two outs against me. Would this third time really be the charm? I couldn't make another marriage mistake.

From the first time I met him, I loved his sense of humor. I noticed how well he treated his mother. I enjoyed watching his courtesies to other people. I appreciated his kindnesses.

We were two older people with parallel experiences and shared values. We learned to meld our lives as capable individuals into a shared life of two people who liked each other and wanted to be together. We formed a friendship as we grew our romance. I learned that the friendship part of the relationship is one of the keys to our daily happiness.

Like any two people, we've had our ups and downs. But we never go to bed angry. I've learned to relax my grip on the reigns of life. I've learned to accept Steve as he is, not as how I want him to be. That was golden for me. We aim to please each other. We don't impose unrealistic expectations on the other. We enjoy our life together. And he is a man big enough to understand why I still use my second husband's last name.

Life is not perfect, but it is pretty darned good. We cannot imagine life without each other. Steve and I begin each day with a cup of coffee and a game of cribbage. We end each day with another game of cribbage and share the events of our day.

We talk. Communication lines are always open. We keep no secrets, except to surprise each other on gift-giving holidays. He is my true partner.

"Live, Laugh, Love" are the three words centered on the wall above the headboard of our bed. Steve and I start each day with a hug and a smile because we are happy with our life together. For me, the third time was the charm.

Nellie Williams, EA, author, speaker, trainer and coach, is The IRS Insider who wants to help you know the rules of the tax game to win. Be happy by turning your panic attack into a plan of attack.

www.BulletProofYourTaxes.com

An Unlikely Purchase

by Ross Wright

I had been dating Annette for about two years when we decided I would rent out my house and move into hers. She was divorced with two kids. We were living in Pasadena in a house she had bought a year after her divorce and about a month before she had met me.

Two years later, she was financially under water. She had tried everything but was going to lose the house. At the time, I was eking out a living as a freelance musician, and what I was able to contribute wasn't nearly enough to stop the foreclosure.

About a year earlier, I had taken a HELOC from my house and invested in real estate. So when a letter from the bank arrived announcing that in two months the house was going to be auctioned for $644,210, I didn't panic. Instead, I got thinking. She had purchased the house for $980,000, the market had dipped a bit, but it was still worth about $900,000. If I could purchase the house at auction for $800,000 or less, we could stay and the kids could finish the school year. Then we could sell the place and recover some of the money she would have otherwise lost.

So, how does a freelance musician with no stable income get an $800,000 loan? The first people we approached were Annette's parents, who promptly said "No!" Since that hadn't worked out so well, I put together a more detailed business plan. Then I began to ask everyone I knew who had money or could get money.

The first person I asked was my friend Steve, who is a very wealthy English businessman. But he wasn't interested in helping and politely told me to piss off. The next person on my list was his ex-wife, Pam. She was very nice and told me that she would love to help but had just invested in a large land deal and could only loan me £100,000. In my mind, I imagined that equaled $200,000, so my new strategy was to find four investors at $200,000 each.

Almost immediately, I got another investor who could put up another $200,000, so I was halfway there. I began to ask everyone I knew.

Monday 2 p.m., two days before the auction, I got another $200,000 from someone who had sold his house a few years before and was just sitting on the money. Immediately after I secured the deal, I called Annette's father again. In the back of my mind, I thought if I could come up with $600,000 he would probably pitch in the last $200,000 if it meant preventing his daughter and grand kids from becoming homeless. He reluctantly offered me $100,000. It wasn't the $800,000, but we were in the game.

Now I had one day to collect $700,000 from the four investors, and one lived on the Island of Jersey in the English Channel—different time zone, different currency. A million things could have gone wrong, but miraculously, by Tuesday night I had $500K in cashier's checks, and the wired money from Jersey Island would be picked up from the bank first thing in the morning on the day of the auction.

The auction was at 9 a.m. on the steps of the Pomona courthouse. The plan was to be at the bank the minute it opened, then get to the auction ASAP. Coincidentally, a US Bank branch had just opened exactly across the street from the courthouse. The £100,000 turned out to be $155,000, fortunately I still had money from my HELOC, so I went to the auction with $690,000.

We were the first to arrive. The auctioneer was just setting up. I had never been to an auction, so I had no idea how it worked. I asked him what I needed to do. He could clearly see that I was distressed. He patiently explained the process. I told him I was there to buy my girlfriend's house; then I said: "Hopefully no one will show up." He assured me the entire courthouse steps would soon be full of people. He asked where the house was located. When I told him Pasadena, he laughed and said, "Those houses are often sold sight unseen before the agents even buy them."

He looked up my address on his computer. Oddly, there was no opening bid amount. I pulled out the paper that the bank had sent me. He explained that the $644.210 was the amount owed. The opening bid can be more or less than that; it's up to the bank. I showed him my $690,000, and he told me he would let me know the opening bid amount as soon as it came online.

About two minutes before the auction began, he said, "Your opening bid is $694,343.22. We were $4,343.22 short. Thankfully, my mom was there. She said, "I can get more money." The auctioneer said, "Great! But if you're not back in time, I can't wait for you." So my mom went off to the bank as I stayed and watched.

When my mom finally returned, we gave the auctioneer a thumbs up. Then the next property was our house. The auctioneer made his announcement: "As a representative of such-and-such-a bank, we are going to purchase this property for the sum of $694,343.23. Would anyone like to offer more?" I stood there in a dazed fog and raised my hand and muttered a noise. The auctioneer looked at me and said, "Is that one penny over the asking amount?" I nodded my head yes and made another noise. He banged the gavel and said, "Sold for $694,343.24."

The point of the story is this: Anytime we are in a situation that seems impossible and hopeless, it's also an opportunity for us to achieve one of our greatest triumphs. When we are clear that failure is not an option, and our purpose and intentions are noble, miracles happen and opportunity opens its arms to us.

———————

Ross Wright has been described by the LA times as a "Modern day Renaissance man, who has created his own musical empire," (Composer, Arranger, Conductor, Bassist, Author, Radio Personality, and Entrepreneur) and is also known as Elvis Schoenberg, the creator of the Orchestre Surreal. He has performed and toured internationally with a wide variety of musical artists, and his compositions have been performed throughout the world.

www.Ross-Wright.com

FROM ABUSE VICTIM TO SURVIVOR AND THRIVER

by Sharyn Yuloff

I was born to a teen who married my 19-year-old father to get out of her dad's house. Stereotypically, she chose a man much like her dad. Three years later, they divorced, and Mom then married my stepfather, and we all moved to Israel when he had to return to university.

I didn't see my dad again until the summer I turned 7, when mom, my one-year-old sister and I returned to Los Angeles to see family, including my dad and his new wife. We clicked so well that I was invited to spend the next summer with him in California.

Soon after I returned from my long stay with dad, the Yom Kippur War broke out. I was so scared that I developed a form of PTSD. I knew of a land that didn't have wars, and my dad lived there, so I relentlessly implored my mom to allow me to leave Israel. On Jan. 7, 1974, I landed at LAX to live with my new family. I was almost nine-years-old and had forgotten most of my Hebrew language skills on the flight.

A few months later over dinner, I received the best news: I was going to have a new baby brother. I was so excited, I couldn't stay seated!

What I didn't know was that adding another child to this family would throw off the delicate balance and tax my father's fragile coping skills. The next seven years were filled with blood or threats thereof and six attempts to find a suitable father figure—most of whom sexually violated me in some way. All this abuse ended when I was 16, with my father's hands around my throat, and me very calmly telling him that he must remove his hands from around my neck (all because I hadn't cleaned the litter box when he thought I should have). Since he did remove his hands, I realized that my brothers (now 7 and 5) were old enough to spend much of their time either in school or after-school care and thus were not relying on me for protection except for the evenings my stepmother was working as an RN.

At about the same time, my mother (who had returned to Los Angeles soon after her now 7-year-old son was born) divorced my stepfather and was living near Dodger Stadium, so I moved in to "help" her.

Over the next years, in addition to finishing school, I spent countless hours reading personal development books, fighting for custody of my father's sons, and cohabiting with the wrong guys…all leading to clinical depression with suicidal plans and a week locked up in a psych ward. I was released after promising to attend regular meetings of a 12-step program called Co-Dependents Anonymous. Not too surprising of an outcome for someone with my abuse history.

Things changed two months after being released. While attending Shabbat Services at a new synagogue, I met the man that three years later would become my husband. It still took decades of psychotherapy, psychotropic drugs, and many years of business education (on the job, an MBA in non-profit management, and years of business development training through numerous MasterMinds) to find a way to realize a lifelong dream.

My stepfather's parents owned and operated an import/export business, and I grew up watching them enjoy a business relationship and a growing family together. Even then, I thought it would be amazing to have that experience when I was married.

Of course, my business life didn't initially lend itself to that kind of intertwining. I started out in teaching, then in accounting, which led to executive assistant, office management, and human resources roles. Unless we could tremendously grow my husband's marketing company, there would be no connection for us to work together—until a few years ago.

I was offered an opportunity as an HR director for a 300-employee company, but that was short lived as they were sold to a huge multinational firm and I was "laid off" 90 days after the acquisition was finalized. Days before my termination, I was advised that a pain I'd been feeling was due to a repetitive strain injury and subject to Workers' Compensation coverage.

Before my disability coverage terminated, one of my husband's clients mentioned that she was thinking about hiring an office manager. I asked her to let me know when she was ready, hoping that the timing and the money would correlate. It did!

She continues to be our ideal open and transparent client. She has literally entrusted me with "the keys to her kingdom." I can hear her voice in my head as I type emails to her clients who never know if she is answering or unavailable. Through that engagement, I earned the title of Online Business Manager and found a way to work on projects with my husband and began to use those skills to build my husband's business and work with him on many projects.

We vacationed several times in Sedona, Arizona, and fantasized about moving our business there. On one trip, my husband had an idea for a new product we could offer to current and prospective clients, and this year we realized that dream and opened Sedona Marketing Retreats, where we help groups and private clients create strategic marketing plans with ongoing marketing coaching.

There are still moments I am triggered and transported back into those early memories, but I've learned to not allow them to stop me from enjoying the relationship we've created and the dream life that is magically transforming before our eyes!

In the interest of space, I've glossed over many important points that led me from abuse victim to survivor. If you would like to talk, you can find me at Sharyn@SedonaMarketing.com.

If, like many others, you seek anonymous assistance, I encourage you to visit the online facilitated chat rooms provided by YesICAN.org ("working to break the silence and cycle of abuse"). I'm a longtime member of their board of directors.

Sharyn Yuloff is an HR and Online Business Manager for the company she co-founded with her husband, Sedona Marketing Retreats. She is a professional speaker, author, and radio co-host (with her husband) of The Marketing Checklist. Sharyn and her husband host marketing retreats for entrepreneurs and small business owners in an exclusive executive retreat setting in Sedona Arizona.

www.SedonaMarketingRetreats.com

CRAIG DUSWALT'S RESOURCES

Craig Duswalt's Events
Craig Duswalt's Personal Growth Weekend
Embrace Your RockStar Life
Every January
www.PersonalGrowthWeekend.com

Craig Duswalt's Marketing BootCamp
How to Achieve RockStar Status in Your Industry
Every March and September
www.CDMarketingBootCamp.com

Craig Duswalt's BOOK Camp
How to Write a Book in 30 Days to Promote Your Business and Get it Published
Every May
www.RockStarBookCamp.com

Craig Duswalt International, Inc.
www.CraigDuswaltMarketing.com

Internet Radio Network
RadioStar Worldwide
www.RadioStarWorldWide.com

Publishing Company
Duswalt Press
www.DuswaltPress.com

Speaker Bureau
RockStar Keynote Speakers
www.RockStarKeynoteSpeakers.com

Shopping Cart
www.RockStarCart.com

Craig Duswalt's MasterMind
Elite community where "RockStars" exchange ideas to grow their Business
and succeed in Life!
Come to any of Craig Duswalt's events to find out more about this unique
membership.

Craig Duswalt's Speaking Topics
How to Achieve RockStar Status in Your Industry
How to Write a Book in 30 Days to Promote Your Business and Get it
Published
College Speaker—How to Achieve *RockStar Status* in College Without
Doing Drugs
To book Craig Duswalt as a speaker at your next event, please call
805-241-8170.